A. H. Ames

The Revelation of Saint John the Divine

An Interpretation

A. H. Ames

The Revelation of Saint John the Divine
An Interpretation

ISBN/EAN: 9783337779320

Printed in Europe, USA, Canada, Australia, Japan

Cover: Foto ©Lupo / pixelio.de

More available books at **www.hansebooks.com**

THE
REVELATION OF ST. JOHN THE DIVINE

AN INTERPRETATION

BY

A. H. AMES, M.D., D.D.

NEW YORK: EATON & MAINS
CINCINNATI: CURTS & JENNINGS

Preface

THE essay which follows is based upon a conviction that the closing book of the canon of the New Testament, known as the Revelation of Saint John, presents the thoughts of that holy man and inspired apostle upon the subject of the kingdom of Christ, as derived by him from the Old Testament Scriptures and from the teachings of Christ or as drawn from direct revelations made to himself. The book presents a single theme and has a well-preserved unity.

With those theories of interpretation which would make of the book an epitome of history, either as confined to particular epochs or as a whole, and which presuppose its design to be the prediction of events, great or small, in the progress of the world or the Church, the writer of this essay is not in sympathy. It is mainly because of the vagaries and conceits to which these theories have opened the way, which have clouded rather than cleared the mysteries

Preface

of the Apocalypse and been more promotive of strife than of salvation, that so many thoughtful and pious minds have been driven from the study of what is one of the most beautiful, as it is one of the most practical, parts of the word of God. How readily the coincidences, for such they are, which have been appealed to as verifications of these theories may be explained and accounted for will be shown in the course of the essay.

Questions of criticism or scholarship do not lie within the scope of the essay. It is assumed, not, however, without examination and reflection, that the Revelation is the work of John, the son of Zebedee, one of the twelve, and "the disciple whom Jesus loved." It is also assumed that he was the author of the fourth gospel and of the epistles which bear his name.

Commentaries upon the Revelation have been so numerous that their titles would fill a volume. It is not likely that anything can be said concerning it which is entirely new and has not been somewhere set forth. The writer of this essay claims originality so far as that he has not seen the views here expressed elsewhere presented, al-

Preface

though they may have appeared previously It is not possible for him to say whence he has gathered the material which has grown into the essay, so as to make formal acknowledgment. Alford, Bengel, Hengstenberg, Wordsworth, *The Speaker's Commentary*, Ellicott's *Commentary*, *The Expositor's Bible* have been consulted freely, and also *The Symbolic Parables of the Apocalypse*, published by T. and T. Clark. The best commentary upon the Revelation he has found to be the Scriptures themselves.

Washington, D. C.

Contents

INTRODUCTION
Rules of Interpretation—The Structure of the Book—Reference to Old Testament—Emblems Interpreted by Light of Jewish Scriptures and Ritual—Particular Attention to Numbers.......................... Pages 1-26

PART I
The Seven Churches of Asia, or the Kingdom as it Actually was in the Days of the Apostles and is Now..... 29-35

PART II
Fundamental Principles on Which the Kingdom is Based—Emblem of the Seals—Opening of the Seals—The Sealed Elect... 39-52

PART III
The Means by which the Kingdom of Christ is Advanced—Natural Providences—The Two Witnesses, or the Supernatural Scriptures........................... 55-97

PART IV
The Foes of the Kingdom—The Dragon—First Wild Beast, or Spirit of Worldliness—Second Wild Beast, or Spirit of False Prophetism—Anticipations of Victory.. 101-166

PART V
The Counterfeit of the Kingdom, or the False Church—The Judgments of God—Vision of the Vials—Babylon and its Doom—Methods of Success Reiterated..... 169-202

Contents

PART VI

Progressive Steps by Which the Ideal Kingdom is to be Realized—Restraints upon the Power of Satan—Outpouring of the Holy Spirit under the Emblem of Resurrection—Union of Christian Believers—Final Triumph over Barbarism under the Emblem of Gog and Magog... 205-258

PART VII

The Ideal of the Kingdom—Its Distinctive Features—The Central Principle of the Kingdom—Negative Characteristics—Fruits and Results.................. 261-276

Introduction

Rules of Interpretation

IF the Revelation of Saint John has any right to a place in the canon of the New Testament, it is reasonable to presume that its intention was to conform to that general purpose for which all divinely inspired Scripture is said to be given, namely, to "be profitable for doctrine, for reproof, for correction, for instruction in righteousness: that the man of God may be perfect, thoroughly furnished unto all good works."

What peculiarly distinguishes it is that it clothes spiritual truth with a garb of mystery which, by challenging investigation, stimulates inquiry; which affords to the mind that solves its obscurities the satisfaction always to be found in the discovery of the recondite and difficult; which throws around prose realities the pleasing charm of poetry and art; and which, by connecting material things with a divine revelation, and thus linking together nature and the supernatural, attests the unity of the uni-

Introduction

verse in which we are placed and shows the world about us and human history to be full of the presence of God.

It would surely argue great presumption in any man to claim a perfect understanding of a book so marvelous as the Apocalypse, whose teachings are not for one age, but for all ages. Very confidently, however, it may be asserted that by the use of certain rules of interpretation many of its mysteries may be explained and its application to practical life and conduct be made evident. The reasonableness of these rules would be readily admitted if applied to any other part of holy writ; and hesitation to accept them here proceeds solely from that mistaken view of the design of the Revelation which isolates it from the rest of the sacred canon as something anomaious and unique. So far is this from being the case that no book in the Bible can afford to stand by itself so little as the Apocalypse, inasmuch as there is no other into the fabric of which so much of the other Scriptures is intentionally woven. The impression which close study of it makes is that it was designed by its author to serve as a sacred clasp to bind together

Introduction

and hold in harmonious coherence the whole of God's wonderful volume.

The principles of interpretation deserving special notice are four in number.

1. *The structure of the book itself furnishes some guide to its interpretation.*

The opening chapters comprise brief letters, seven in all, which the author is directed to write to seven churches of Asia, the number indicating, not that these comprehended all the churches in that region, but that in them were represented all phases of religious life. These letters set before us both the spiritual state and the environment of the churches, and are advisory, monitory, reproachful, or comforting as the cases demanded.

The closing chapters present us with a picture of the perfected Christian Church— a symbolical vision, incomparable in its exquisite beauty, of the complete and permanent triumph of the Gospel of Christ, in the individual heart and on the larger field of the world, over all opposing forces; the realization, in fact, on earth of the ideal kingdom of God made ready for the Lamb.

The most plausible suggestion, therefore, which presents itself is that the intermediate

Introduction

portion of the book is intended to present in its figures and symbols the means by which the last condition is to be reached from the earlier one, the unformed and fluctuating state of the beginning developed into the ripeness and perfection of the close, and that under the guise of metaphor, trope, and vision there are revealed to us the dangers which the Church of Christ must expect, the enemies it must subdue, the weapons by which victory must be achieved, the encouragements upon which it may rely, and, in short, the steps through which the immature and carnal must be led in order to reach up to the pure and perfect.

Nor is it with the Church at large that the warnings and counsels have alone to do. If "whatsoever things were written aforetime were written for our learning," each individual disciple of Christ may find in this book a chart for his own life's journey and have sufficient warning against the sunken rocks, the adverse tides, the dangerous headlands which are to be shunned, and which are here so clearly and plainly marked out for him that he may, in the close and careful study of the map, find equal profit and pleasure.

Introduction

It is very important in this connection to note the statement of the writer in the first verse of the book, that his commission was "to show unto" the servants of God "things which must shortly come to pass." It is only by a very forced construction of the words that they can be made to signify a prophecy whose fulfillment is to be delayed for long centuries indefinite in their number. The most natural construction surely is that the revelation intrusted to him is one of which the whole, and not a part only, is to find its application in the times in which he lived, or soon thereafter, and to continue applicable until the glorious result is attained of which the closing part speaks. And if we shall dismiss from our minds all prepossessions springing out from that view of the book which makes it a syllabus, or table of contents, of Christian history the force of this remark will more clearly appear.

2. *Reference must constantly be made to the Old Testament.*

This rule, which is of importance in order to understand any part of the New Testament, becomes of the highest necessity in any attempt to interpret the Revelation.

Introduction

The writer was evidently a diligent student of the older Scriptures, absorbing their images and emblems until they had become a part of himself. Much in his writings that at first seems obscure becomes plain when we put ourselves in his position and study the Scriptures, which were evidently in his thoughts.

The prophetical books of the Old Testament especially are to be studied. Between the relation in which the older prophets stood to the laws and institutions of Moses and that which the apostles of the New Testament dispensation sustained to the Lord Jesus Christ a strong similarity exists. Neither the one nor the other claimed to be originators or independent discoverers, but rather witnesses to truths already revealed, which they accepted as primary and fundamental facts. Into the clear understanding, indeed, of these they were enabled by divine inspiration to look more deeply than others could, and they were also supernaturally aided to draw them out into great principles, capable of application to human thought and conduct in the shaping of individual and national life and practice. Thus, naturally and by sympathy of

Introduction

condition, the later writers found themselves led into careful and profound study of their predecessors. The prophecies of Daniel and Zechariah deserve to be especially consulted. Written, as they were, at or near the time of the captivity of Judah, they had peculiar interest for one who was himself an exile for the truth. Some of the imagery of the Revelation is drawn from the glowing poetry of Isaiah. And almost the entire Book of Joel has been worked into the Apocalypse.

But of all helps to an understanding of the Revelation the most fruitful is a close and careful comparison with the Book of Ezekiel; especially is this the case in reference to the closing chapters of both. Between the authors of these two works there were striking similarities of character and condition. But a more powerful bond of union is found in the fact that both of them were preëminently prophets of the Holy Spirit, seeming to have reached truer and profounder views of his work in the economy of redemption than any predecessors in their separate dispensations. Isaiah and Paul wrote of Christ and his Church; but if we wish to learn the fullest development

Introduction

of the office of the Holy Ghost we must turn to the pages of Ezekiel and John.

In addition to the Old Testament references, the prophetical discourses of our Lord uttered near the close of his ministry and recorded in the synoptical gospels will throw much light on the Book of Revelation. The omission of these from the gospel of John may be accounted for by the fact that in the Revelation the apostle had made such large use of them. The important prediction of Paul concerning the man of sin, found in 2 Thess. ii, must also be compared with those of John.

3. *The emblems and symbols of the Revelation must be interpreted by the light of the Jewish Scriptures and ritual.*

This, indeed, follows as a corollary form the preceding rule, but is of so much importance as to deserve special mention. Sometimes a word or a figure of speech or the connections of a sentence or a passing allusion to some sacrificial service will afford a clew to what at the time was in the mind of the writer. Inasmuch as he was a Jew, "taught according to the perfect manner of the law of the fathers," familiar with the Scriptures, traditions, usages, and history

Introduction

of his religion, his interpretation of symbols and emblems would naturally be such as would occur to the mind of a Jew. We must place ourselves as near as possible to his standpoint. Yet, as he was also an inspired apostle of the Lord Jesus Christ, we must be prepared to concede that he read deeper into these mysteries than his fellows did and was able to import into them a richer meaning.

4. *Particular attention must be given to the numbers found in the book.*

Much that is fanciful and extravagant has, it must be conceded, been written on this subject, and to many persons any discussion of it is distasteful. Yet it is certain, as the Wisdom of Solomon says, that God has "ordered all things in measure and number and weight." Otherwise there could be no such thing as exact science. Truths lie veiled in figures, for these represent fixed principles and plans in the divine mind. As a general truth, it may be stated that the ideas expressed by numbers, not only in this book, but throughout the Bible, whenever these are used symbolically, are those of fullness, exactness, and perfection, on one hand, or deficiency, incompleteness, and imperfection, on the other.

Introduction

The numbers which figure most largely in symbolism are seven, twelve, six, and three and a half.

Seven is called the sacred number, and seems to express the idea of perfection or fullness to the highest degree and in the most unlimited sense. As seven days make a complete week, whole and entire, without redundancy or deficiency, so that to which the number seven is attached must be taken as perfect, fully developed, as a complete whole. The expressions "seven spirits," "seven seals," "seven trumpets," etc., imply that what they represent must be taken as entire, with no possible capacities lying in them unexhausted.

Twelve, also, signifies completeness; but its use and application are more restricted. It is usually connected with the Church of God, and possibly has some special reference to it. Thus there are twelve patriarchs, twelve apostles, twelve foundations to the holy city. As the number is formed by the multiplication of three, representing the Trinity, and four, representing the world with its quarters, it conveys the thought of universality as the assured destiny of the Church.

Introduction

Six is, also, as a symbol, connected with the Church; but, both because it is less than seven, and only the half of twelve, has a sinister significance. It represents the malign and baleful influences which corrupt and disintegrate the Church, shearing it of its power, limiting and obstructing its mission, and leaving it incomplete, defective, and corrupt.

Three and a half is a number having special signification and requiring particular investigation. A correct appreciation of its meaning will throw light upon some of the most obscure portions of the Apocalypse.

It occurs—and is, indeed, the only number of which this may be said—in various forms. Since three and a half years comprise forty-two months, and since forty-two months of thirty days each (the usual prophetical computation) equal twelve hundred and sixty days, we may take these three forms, three and a half, forty-two, and twelve hundred and sixty, as equivalent expressions. So, also, the expression, "a time, times, and the dividing of times" ($1+2+\frac{1}{2}=3\frac{1}{2}$), is probably but another form of this number. That some law governs the choice of these various forms is probable; but what, it is does not appear.

Since three and a half falls short of seven, it designates incompleteness. But, inasmuch as it is the exact half of seven (in this differing from six), it signifies an incompleteness which has, so to speak, a completeness of its own—that is, an incompleteness which is not anomalous and irregular, such as would be expressed by six, but one which is, by the appointment of God or as a result of its own nature, intended to be such. Any period of time or epoch in human history which has prescribed and well-marked limits or boundaries, any part of the plan of Providence which has a specified, but only temporary and partial purpose as related to the whole course and complete plan of the divine Being, is always designated by one or the other of the forms of this number.

Judaism, for instance, answered these conditions. It was a providentially ordered dispensation, but with a specific and limited object; fulfilling a definite, but not the complete purpose of Providence; a stage in the movement of humanity toward the kingdom of God, but not itself the realization of that kingdom; a type which needed an antitype to round it out, and throughout which ran the marks that proved it to be only temporary and preparatory to a higher dispensation into which it was to blossom. It was "a schoolmaster to bring us unto Christ." Its glory was something which was "to be done away," and consequently falls short of "that which remaineth." And it reached the "fullness" of its "time" when "God sent forth his Son, made of a woman, made under the law, to redeem them that were under the law, that we might receive the adoption of sons." And it will be found that whenever Judaism is symbolized by a number in the Book of Revelation, it is designated by one of the allotropic forms of three and a half.*

So, likewise, Gentilism, to which a definite and distinct character or purpose is attributed, both by our Lord (Luke xxi, 24) and by Saint Paul (Rom xi, 25), but which, when severed from its Jewish antecedents, has the like features of incompleteness and deficiency, would be symbolically expressed by some form of the same number.†

So generally accepted seems to have been

* See Rev. xi, 3; xii, 6, 14.   † See Rev. xiii, 5.

Introduction

this symbolical use of numbers that it appears even in such pure and simple prose as the gospels. The evangelist Matthew, in recording the genealogy of our Lord, divides the period between Abraham and Christ into three cycles with fourteen generations in each, or forty-two in all. This period is exactly coeval with Judaism as a distinct dispensation; and forty-two is, as we have seen, one of the interchangeable forms of the number three and a half. Inasmuch as the actual number of generations was, as is generally agreed, more than forty-two, and some principle of accommodation must have controlled the evangelist in choosing it, we have a right to conjecture that the symbolism was so well established that no erroneous impression would be conveyed.

Using these rules of interpretation as a guide, it will be found that many, if not most of the obscurities which have made this book so perplexing and incomprehensible will be removed. A unity of purpose will be seen pervading it. It will no longer appear anomalous and *outré*, but harmonious with the rest of the oracles of God; a book for the perusal of every individual be-

Introduction

liever, no matter how simple and unlearned he may be; having direct reference to his heart-experience and his moral conduct; a *vade mecum* for the journey of life through whose aid he may safely encounter the dangers and surely overcome the hindrances he may meet.

The great theme which the inspired writer and apostle here sets before us is the mediatorial kingdom of our Lord Jesus Christ. The principles which lie at the basis of that kingdom—the oppositions, external and internal, to its beginning and completion, the agencies, divine and human, upon which reliance must be placed to achieve success, its superiority to and triumph over all hostile forces, and all these both in the heart of each individual Christian and in that aggregation of Christians which we call the Church—are here delineated as they were revealed to Saint John.

The theories which make of this book an anticipation of history, and which find in the events of the last nineteen centuries continued fulfillments of its predictions, or which confine those fulfillments to the periods either near the primitive age or near the future and final scenes of the

Introduction

drama of time are regarded as being not wholly erroneous, but incomplete and partial.

That the great purposes of divine Providence are continually finding their fulfillment in the history of men and nations is a truth not confined to this book, but spread throughout all the sacred Scriptures. The laws of the divine administration are very exact; they can be neither obeyed nor disregarded without the necessary accompaniments of legitimate and appointed consequences. There is no improbability at all that moral and spiritual truths may have their processes and cycles of development, just as natural things have their seasons and times of maturity. Whether the events that have occurred, the organized bodies, secular or religious, that have appeared on the field of the world, were in the mind of the apostle as he wrote is a question neither affirmed nor denied. What is meant to be said is that the Revelation does more than merely predict results. It goes down into the profound region of causes and reveals the continuity of the plans of the divine Being. However ingenious or plausible, therefore, the explanations put upon the

Introduction

prophecies of this book by the theories spoken of above, it is not confined to them. As long as the world lasts there will be, in every age and in the experience of every believer, a fulfillment of the truths here set forth. Its warnings and comforts will never be out of date. Its promises and its threats are alike imperishable, for they are a part of that "word of our God" which "shall stand forever."

A definition of the phrase "kingdom of Christ" is nowhere attempted in the Revelation. It was not needed in an age when the theme was the staple of preaching and teaching. To show that it must not be confounded with the visible Church was the purpose of the epistles to the churches of Asia with which the Apocalypse begins. The fundamental principle upon which the kingdom is founded, the universal sovereignty of Christ based upon his redemptive work, is taught under the emblem of the seals. The writer then advances to the instrumentalities, natural and supernatural, by means of which the kingdom is to be brought to its consummation. The antagonisms which the kingdom must encounter from foes without and within are next plainly revealed, and, lest the revelation may cause discouragement, prophecies of sure and final victory mingle with warnings. The retributive resources of the kingdom, the just judgments which fall upon its foes, and especially upon the false and counterfeit Church, are taught under the emblem of the vials. The next section discloses to us the stages of progress through which the kingdom ascends to its complete establishment, and the signs by which we may test its advance or detect its decline. And finally, with that glowing picture of the ideal kingdom as it shall be realized on earth when the Galilean shall have conquered, a picture so beautiful that our highest conceptions of heaven seem embodied in it, the divine seer closes his rapturous vision.

PART I
The Seven Churches of Asia

Revelation of Saint John the Divine

PART I

The Seven Churches of Asia, or, the Kingdom as it Actually was in the Days of the Apostles and is now

THE chapters which contain the epistles to the churches of Asia need not detain us long; not that they are devoid of interest, but because anything like a commentary upon the text lies outside the scope and design of this essay, whose purpose is to interpret the general intent of the book itself.

The value of these letters to us lies in the pictures presented in them of the religious state of the churches to which they were addressed, and which doubtless were representative of the Christian world in the days of the writer. The reading of them will dispel any illusion in which we may have indulged as to the superiority of the apostolical age over subsequent ones, and will shatter any hypothesis we may have formed that primitive Christianity was anything like Utopia. The condition of the churches which they reveal to us was one in which doubt and faith, loyalty and declension, purity and worldliness, evil and good were interspersed in varying proportions. The tares had already begun to grow with the wheat.

And a moment's reflection will convince us that no other result could reasonably be expected. Divine grace does not obliterate human nature, and its operations are always in accordance with rule. The regeneration of a soul is not synonymous with its entire sanctification. Growth is an invariable accompaniment of life. It would have been a new and altogether anomalous state of things if the average of conduct attained by converts from Jewish and pagan standards of thought and morals had equaled that to which we may aspire in whom centuries of training in the family, the State, and the Church have created a Christian consciousness. Fervor and zeal the early disciples unquestionably had, but with sad mixture of inconsistency, inexperience, and weakness.

It has always seemed hard for Christians

to comprehend and fully believe the promise which our Lord gave to the Church through the apostles, that the Holy Ghost, when he should come, should "abide" with it "forever." And this abiding presence throughout all ages of the Spirit of truth is not to be in partial or transient manifestation, but in all the fullness of his divine offices. And attention must be called to the fact that John, in unfolding the processes and forces by which the kingdom of Christ is to be brought to its triumphant completeness, points us at the beginning of his prophecy (Rev. iv, 5) to the seven spirits of God "burning before the throne," as if to impress upon us the perfection of degree in which the Holy Spirit gives himself to this work. This does not mean that there is monotonous identity in the modes of his manifestation, or that the work that he does is the same in kind with that which he has done in the past. We are expressly told that "there are diversities of gifts, but the same spirit. And there are diversities of administrations, but the same Lord. And there are diversities of operations, but it is the same God that worketh all in all." Some things which God does he never repeats. His special presence or work at some periods and in some things does not imply that he is any the less, while not in the same special way, present at all times and in all things.

"In the beginning God created the heaven and the earth." That was done once for all. From that period up to this time, indeed, the "Father worketh;" but it is not as Creator, but as Providence, developing and evolving from that beginning the possibilities that lay in it. What we call science is the record of this development, aiming only at the accurate presentation of the facts of providence and the adaptation of them to human needs and destiny. Nature is the *terminus ad quem* toward which discovery and invention tend, not the *terminus a quo* from which they start. Progress in them does not mean adding anything to nature or superseding it or leaving it behind and moving to something beyond it, but merely approaching closer to it, bringing us to better knowledge of and fuller acquaintance with it.

So, likewise, that inspiration of the Holy Ghost by which holy men of God were moved to speak and write what was specially

The Seven Churches of Asia

revealed to them is never to be repeated. The lines along which and the limits within which the Christian Church is to be led were laid down once for all, as those of nature also were. The work of the Spirit now is that of a Providence to bring to realization the ideal then foreshadowed; and in doing this he has divine freedom to breathe where and when he listeth. Pentecost was the commencement of a process of which the closing chapters of the Revelation disclose the completion. And in order to attain this end the perpetual presence and indwelling of the Holy Spirit are promised in all their richness and perfection, but in accordance with the laws of human nature and with constant increments of knowledge and power.

It is vain, therefore, to claim commanding authority for any ceremony, formula, or organization on the ground that it corresponds with primitive Christianity. The apostles never felt themselves bound to that first sketch of the Church which they drew at Pentecost, as if this were among the things supernaturally revealed; but they modified and revised it whenever they could say, "It seemed good to the Holy

Ghost and to us." Nor have we any reason to believe that the process of evolution which continued throughout their lives ended therewith. The Holy Spirit did not then cease his work of guidance and inspiration. That is the truest and most apostolical Christianity which, like John, being "in the Spirit on the Lord's day," holds itself ever ready to hear and obey the "great voice, as of a trumpet," behind and above it.

And this is the lesson we are to learn from the seven epistles to the churches of Asia. They are the record of the beginning of the kingdom of Christ, repeated in the conversion and regeneration of every individual Christian. They show the point of departure from which progress is to be made toward the consummation and perfection of the ideal. The Christian world as it was then, with its graces and its faults, is disclosed to us. The apostle, with his clearer eye, was able to look below the facts and recognize the principles struggling for the ascendency; and, using these facts as his *data*, he drew from them a prophecy of the development of the kingdom of Christ of marvelous interest and instruction for all subsequent ages. Nor is there a single force, friendly or hostile to the kingdom, which does not appear in the warnings or encouragements he is directed to write to these infant churches. Whoever will take the sketch of the kingdom as it actually appeared to the eye of John, and contrast it with the culmination of the process so exquisitely pictured in the last two chapters of the Apocalypse, will have some conception of the field over which he must travel if he would "come in the unity of the faith, and of the knowledge of the Son of God, unto a perfect man, unto the measure of the stature of the fullness of Christ."

PART II

Fundamental Principles on which the Kingdom is Based

PART II

Fundamental Principles on which the Kingdom is Based. Emblem of the Seals

WITH the fourth chapter the symbolical part of the Revelation begins, and continues to the end of the book. In that portion of it upon which we now enter, and which includes chapters iv–viii, 1, the emblem of a seal is employed so frequently as to make it the distinctive feature. We are told of a book "sealed with seven seals" which none but the Lamb is worthy to open. Then we are told of the opening of these seals, with visions accompanying the successive loosing of them. And, lastly, a specific number of persons sealed in their foreheads are shown us, following which an innumerable company is seen gathered before the throne of God. It behooves us to ascertain the typical meaning of a seal; and if we succeed in so doing the purpose of the writer will be disclosed.

1. *The Emblem of the Seals.*—The seal has been usually taken as signifying concealment or secrecy; sealed things have been regarded as synonymous with hidden things.

And very much conjecture has been offered as to what were the hidden mysteries contained in the sealed book or scroll. But, whatever secondary meaning the seal may have, concealment is not its principal one. A seal denotes, primarily and specifically, ownership, not secrecy. The sealing of anything implies that it is, or is claimed to be, the property of him who affixes the seal. The outward stamp is the declaration that the owner makes of his rights and is the official token of his authority. It is the mark of lordship or seigniority. Any concealment of contents therein involved is a secondary consideration.

Some illustrations from Scripture will substantiate this interpretation.

When it is said (Rom. iv, 11) that Abraham received "the sign of circumcision, a seal of the righteousness of the faith which he had," it is meant that he then became in a special sense the personal property of Almighty God and entitled to all the protection of Omnipotence.

"He that hath received his testimony hath set to his seal ['hath set his seal to this,' Revised Version] that God is true" (John iii, 33), means that the assured con-

Fundamental Principles

viction of God's reality and faithfulness has become the personal possession of the believer, something which belongs to him of right.

"Him hath God the Father sealed" (John vi, 27) means that God officially ratifies and acknowledges as his own what Christ does, and attests it with the stamp of authority.

When Pilate sealed the sepulcher where Christ was laid (Matt. xxvii, 66) it was meant that the tomb became the property of the Roman empire and was under the guardianship of its officials, and that whoever tampered with it must be prepared to try questions with Cæsar.

"Ye were sealed with that Holy Spirit" (Eph. i, 13) means that ye received as your own possession, in your own personal experience, the earnest of your inheritance; the gift of the Holy Spirit attests your rightful claim to it.

These examples will suffice to indicate the scriptural meaning of the seal. We have only to apply this meaning to the solution of the problem before us. "A book written within and on the back side," that is, completely, all over, with no blank or empty space, is seen lying in the right hand of God on the throne. Plainly, this book with its contents signifies something over which the divine Being asserts supreme sovereignty, which he claims as his of right and alone. And the number of the seals—seven—indicates that this sovereignty is complete, undivided, perfect.

What the contents of the book were we may infer from the preceding chapter (iv), in which we are shown the court of the Lord God omnipotent, with his loyal and obedient servants and hierarchies worshiping him and saying, "Thou hast created all things, and for thy pleasure they are and were created." The book with its seals is a symbol of the fundamental truth of all truths, that all things and beings in this universe, whatever and wherever they are, belong originally and normally to the Creator. His sovereignty over his creatures is absolute, illimitable, and eternal.

It is quite in accordance with John's cast of mind (and this furnishes no slight evidence as to the authorship of the Revelation) in unfolding to us the plan of redemption to take his stand at that period in the past, far back and without date, when God was all in all, and when sin had not entered to dispute his supremacy; just as in his gospel he commences, not with the Christ in the maturity of his powers, or even incarnate in the flesh, but with the preëxistent Word who was "in the beginning," "was with God," and " was God." Profoundest of all the apostles, his mind reveled in the contemplation of beginnings and ends, of the primeval origin and final consummation of things, of the alpha and omega of creation.

But along with this vision of sovereignty came the coincident remembrance of the universe as it is, disordered and in rebellion; of a sinful world wandering from its orbit, disputing the supremacy of its Maker and God, and in unequal and hopeless conflict with Omnipotence. Into whose possession should it pass, and who could assume the reins of power which seemed to have fallen from the hands of the Creator?

A thought similar to this appears to have passed through the mind of Isaiah when he turned from the vision of the throne " high and lifted up," with the seraphim veiling their faces in the presence of holy Majesty, to the spectacle of himself and the world, and cried, " Woe is me! for I am undone."

So John "wept much" when, after this view of immaculate purity combined with almightiness, he contemplated a sinful world powerless to dispute what it would not willingly obey. Who was there worthy to "open the book" and to "loose the seals thereof," and thus to bring back creatures to their rightful allegiance? If they would not submit, yet could not resist, the result could be only disaster, for the heavens must rule, and successful rebellion was impossible.

But there came to John hope and help, as there had come also to Isaiah; and to both from "the altar." As John looked he beheld the "Lion of the tribe of Judah," but in the form of a "Lamb as it had been slain," take the book from the right hand of God and proceed to break the seals.

Now, if a seal is the emblem of ownership it follows that the authorized and permitted loosing of a seal must mean the transference, or delegation, of proprietorship. And this is the meaning here. There is an endowment—donation, rather—of authority, and the change in possession is published. That which belonged to and had been under the rule of the Father is consigned to and becomes the possession of the Son. And the change is not simply one of sovereigns, but of the ground principle of sovereignty; not only of rulers, but of methods of rule. The song of the "elders" and "living creatures" is now, not "Thou didst create," but "Thou hast redeemed us to God by thy blood." There is presented to us, in fact, a picture of the mediatorial sovereignty of the Son of God. We see the inauguration of the kingdom of Christ, the fundamental principle of which is, "Ye are not your own;" for "ye are bought with a price: therefore glorify God." It was written in the Psalms, "The Lord hath said unto me, Thou art my Son; this day have I begotten thee. Ask of me, and I shall give thee the heathen for thine inheritance, and the uttermost parts of the earth for thy possession." John was looking upon the fulfillment of that decree.

Of this mediatorial kingdom of Christ, thus presented to us in symbol, so much is said in the Bible that only a few texts need to be referred to out of the many which might be cited. Our Lord himself said of it that the Father "hath committed all judgment unto the Son" (John v, 22). And again, "All things are delivered unto me of my Father" (Matt. xi, 27). And still again, "All power is given unto me in heaven and in earth" (Matt. xxviii, 18). So in Heb. ii, 8, it is recorded, "Thou hast put all things in subjection under his feet." And Paul has written, "Then cometh the end, when he shall have delivered up the kingdom to God, even the Father; when he shall have put down all rule and all authority and power. For he must reign, till he hath put all enemies under his feet" (1 Cor. xv, 24, 25).

2. *The Opening of the Seals.*—In the exercise of his sovereignty the mediating and atoning Lamb assumes the authority committed to him, and the history of redemption begins. We approach the heart of this wonderful book, and its great purpose begins to reveal itself. But the unfolding of that history has been so different from the conception of it that was possible even to an apostle that "blindness in part" would happen to us all if we had not the revelation of God's plans made known to us in order to check despondency and animate to labor.

John was one of those to whom the Master had said, "Behold, I send you forth."

He had heard and has recorded the prayer of the great High Priest, "As thou hast sent me into the world, even so have I also sent them into the world." He had received the great commission, "Go ye therefore, and teach all nations." He had been taught that Christians were to be "the salt of the earth" and "the light of the world" and were to "occupy" until Christ comes again. What expectation more reasonable could he entertain than that redemption, proceeding from the heart of the Father, consummated in the sacrifice of the Son, and applied by the ever-abiding Spirit, would move forward without let or hindrance from its commencement to its glorious realization? And this is implied in the vision of the opening of the first seal: "Behold a white horse: and he that sat on him had a bow; and a crown was given unto him: and he went forth conquering, and to conquer." The first stroke of God's providence always drives the kingdom well forward. It is the subsequent ones that try men's faith.

When the promise of the seed which should bruise the serpent's head was given to Eve, and, following that, a son was born to her, was it not natural that, in the fullness of her faith, she should exclaim, "I have gotten a man from the Lord?"

When Almighty God, who had just beaten down Pharaoh and Amalek and written the law with his own fingers, said to Moses, "As truly as I live, all the earth shall be filled with the glory of the Lord," could the prophet have any doubt that the ark of the covenant would move triumphantly onward until it came to perfect rest in Canaan?

There is much to show that the apostles of Christ anticipated the speedy conquest of the world by his kingdom. The conversion of thousands at Pentecost, the multitude of accessions which followed, the obedience of a great company of priests, the appearance of miracles all conspired to foster this expectation. The morning hour of every reformation is brignt and golden. It is later on that clouds gather and the skies darken. Painful realities soon shake men out of such sunny dreams, and banish such fond illusions as did the murder of Abel, the lusting after the fleshpots of Egypt, the imprisonment of Peter, the defection of Ananias, the martyrdom of Stephen and James. And as the pendulum of hope swings so easily to the extreme of despair, and every little Ai seems

Fundamental Principles

to our alarmed imagination a walled Jericho, nothing can be conceived more helpful to faith and courage than to learn that such things must needs be, and to be comforted at the same time with the assurance that, though in the world we shall have tribulation, yet Christ has overcome the world and we must not lose heart.

This is the purpose for which the visions accompanying the opening of the seals were given to John. The second seal signifies war; the third, famine; the fourth, pestilence; the fifth, martyrdom; the sixth, revolutions that seem to "shake the heavens, and the earth, and the sea, and the dry land." These are strange instruments to do God's will, unlooked-for messengers to perform his bidding. But not only all things, but all events as well, are under the sovereignty of Christ; and in spite of these obstacles, and perhaps by means of them, his kingdom moves forward. And when the seventh and last seal shall be broken, when every messenger shall have been delegated, when the last needed encouragement shall have been given and the last enemy destroyed, then will come the unbroken and eternal Sabbath of rest.

3. *The Sealed Elect.*—The third part of this section comprises two visions: first, of the "hundred and forty and four thousand," out of the twelve tribes of Israel, sealed in their foreheads; and, then, of a great multitude out of all nations and peoples, clothed in white robes and bearing palms in their hands. The purpose of these visions is to show that God's ownership extends, not only to things and events, but to persons as well. "The Lord knoweth them that are his."

There need not be any hesitation in interpreting these visions as referring to Jewish and Gentile Christians respectively. The same distinction between the two is made in chap. xiv, 1–6, where the hundred and forty-four thousand who stand on Mount Zion singing a song which no others could learn, namely, the song of Moses and the Lamb, are marked off from those in every nation and people to whom the angel flies with the everlasting Gospel.

It is not meant, surely, that the number one hundred and forty-four thousand is to be taken in an absolutely literal sense. The definite number in all probability stands for a great multitude. How large the number

Fundamental Principles

of believing Israelites was in the days of the apostle we have no means of determining. That it was large may be fairly inferred from Acts xxi, 20. And in the great day of accounts the number may be seen to be beyond our largest calculation.

Still less are we authorized to impute this separation of Jew from Gentile to any national exclusiveness on the part of John. No apostle of the circumcision was any more emphatic than was Paul, the apostle of the Gentiles, in asserting that the order of salvation is, first, the Jew, then, the Gentile, and that "God hath not cast away his people which he foreknew," although "blindness in part is happened to Israel, until the fullness of the Gentiles be come in." And what part the Jew may yet play in bringing about that fullness no man is able to predict.

Moreover, there is no inferiority implied in the privileges and graces which the great multitude enjoys as compared with the sealed elect. They are kings and priests unto God; they are clothed with the robes of victory and joy. And the images by which their nearness to Christ and their participation in the fullest measure of nourishment, safety, and felicity are expressed are not elsewhere exceeded in the Revelation. The description of their triumph seems to anticipate the consummation of the ideal kingdom of Christ, with which the closing chapters of the Apocalypse are replete.

PART III
The Means by which the Kingdom of Christ is Advanced

PART III

The Means by which the Kingdom of Christ is Advanced—Emblem of the Trumpet

THE section of the Revelation which begins with chap. viii, 2, and closes with chap. xi, is characterized by the symbol of the trumpet. In the interpretation of this symbol the key to the understanding of the section must be found. It must not be inferred, because the vision of the trumpets follows that of the seals, that it designates events subsequent to the latter. The seals themselves, as we have seen, are not intended to be predictions of historical events, but strictly emblems of truths or principles; and the trumpets must be in like manner regarded. Succession, coincidence, or any other relation of time has no necessary connection with them. They represent varying phases of the kingdom of Christ, and their relation thereto is the only one that need be regarded.

The trumpet was a familiar instrument in the ritual of Judaism, having a well-known and prescribed use, and is frequently referred to in the Scriptures. The mention of the word would readily suggest to the mind of a Jew its symbolic import, and the writer of the Apocalypse doubtless employed it in this sense.

The trumpet was used as a means of summons. When an assembly was to be gathered, when an alarm was to be given, when a message was to be communicated, it was by the trumpet that attention was arrested and a hearing enforced. It signified that tidings were to be delivered to which it behooved men to listen. It increased the range of the unassisted human voice, with the difference that, while the intensifying of the sound through the use of the instrument carried it over larger spaces, there was a loss of that delicacy, flexibility, and capacity to convey emotions which belong to the unaided human organs of speech.

It was by the trumpet, sounding long and loud, that Jehovah announced his presence at Sinai to Moses and the awe-stricken people, and bade them prepare to receive his law. It was by the blowing of trumpets that the approach of the jubilee year was announced—that very striking type of the redemption purchased by Christ. When the Israelites were marching around Jericho "seven priests bearing seven trumpets of rams' horns" went before the ark of the Lord; and on the seventh day, when, "at the seventh time," the priests blew with the trumpets, the walls fell. And the prophet Joel says, " Blow the trumpet in Zion, sanctify a fast, call a solemn assembly: gather the people." So familiarly has this symbolism passed over into the Christian Church that the preaching of salvation is very commonly spoken of as the blowing of the Gospel trumpet.

If the seals emblematize the truth that all things belong of right to Christ as Mediator, the question very naturally follows, How is this *de jure* ownership to be made a *de facto* one, and what instruments are put into the hands of the Church to enable it to establish the kingdom of Christ on earth? The vision of the trumpets is designed to be the answer to this question.

The trumpets, then, signify the instrumentalities by which men are called to the kingdom of Christ, or the measures which the divine Being employs to advance that kingdom. Their number, seven, indicates that these measures are complete and comprehensive, including every available resource and employing all possible methods of approach to man. God avails himself of every legitimate device to constrain a sinful world to accept the proffer of salvation ere he passes from chastisement and correction to retributive and final judgment. Thus those who reject the offer will be found without excuse, and the despisers of the wedding garment will be stricken speechless in the day of accounts.

The sounding of the trumpets, it will be noticed, is preceded by the "prayers of the saints;" for that "the effectual fervent prayer of a righteous man availeth much" with God is one of the fundamental facts of the kingdom (Psalm xviii, 6–17). And the token of the hearing of the prayers is seen in the "voices, and thunderings, and lightnings, and an earthquake" that followed when the seven angels with the trumpets prepared to sound. The vision doubtless recalled to John's mind the remembrance of that day when, as the disciples prayed, "the place was shaken where they were assembled together;" God revealing himself in the new dispensation as he had done at Sinai when about to communicate his law. The grandeur of the preparation suggests the importance of the tidings to be communicated.

It will be also observed that the episode of the "two witnesses" (chap. xi) falls within the section marked by the trumpet emblem. The appropriateness of this and the ease with which it takes its place here furnish no slight evidence that the explanation of the Revelation adopted in this essay is correct.

There are two modes by which the divine Being has chosen to communicate the knowledge of himself and of his will. These are his works and his word. The one is that manifestation of himself in nature of which Paul speaks when he says, "The invisible things of him from the creation of the world are clearly seen, being understood by the things that are made, even his eternal power and Godhead." The other is supernatural, the revelation of himself as a power above nature and not limited by its laws. It is of this that Peter says, "We have also a more sure word of prophecy."

The most searching and subtle analysis to which knowledge and its sources have been subjected has resulted in this—that even in the alembic of modern doubt, after the most biting acids have tried their solvent power, there is left as the residuum a conviction that, besides this known and knowable universe, there exists a first cause or force. At the beginning and basis of all things a duality must be acknowledged. If human thought by its unaided light is incompetent to go beyond this, it is not allowed to stop short of it. "The momentum of thought," Herbert Spencer says, "inevitably carries us beyond conditioned existence to unconditioned existence." "The certainty that, on the one hand, such a power exists, while, on the other, its nature transcends intuition and is beyond imagination, is the certainty toward which intelligence has been from the first progressing. To this conclusion science inevitably arrives as it reaches its confines." This power, which science may know only as "an infinite and eternal energy," is the Being whom the Scriptures reveal to us as the Lord God, of whom and through whom and to whom "are all things: to whom be glory forever."

From this first Cause knowledge comes to us through two channels—his deeds and his words. The first of these is accessible to all mankind; for the Gentiles, which have not the law, "show the work of the law written in their hearts, their conscience also bearing witness." But as that which is constant and habitual soon ceases to attract attention, and the orderly and uniform processes of nature excite less interest and awaken feebler curiosity than the anomalous and occasional, in like manner it is most frequently by calamities, adversities, seeming withdrawals of God's face that men are brought to reflection, consideration, and obedience. "When thy judgments are in the earth, the inhabitants of the world will learn righteousness." It is this truth that the vision of the trumpets symbolizes. It signifies the warnings in the field of natural providence which the divine Being gives to men, in order to show the evil and peril of sin and thus draw back their souls from the pit. The second of these channels of knowledge is found in the oracles of God, the Scriptures committed to the chosen people. And these are symbolized in the episode of the "two witnesses," which forms a part of the trumpet section.

The details of the trumpet scenes are not, it must be confessed, easy of interpretation.

They seem to be selected from various parts of the Old Testament, and grouped according to some plan not explained to us, suggesting the thought that the interpretation of them is not to be found in any single event, but in some common truth embodied in many events.

The conjunction of "hail" with "fire" (viii, 7) is also found in Exod. ix, 24; that of "fire" with "blood" (viii, 7) in Joel ii, 30; while all three of these elements are separately mentioned in many passages. The moving of mountains (viii, 8) is referred to in Psalm xlvi, 2, and Isa. liv, 10; and a burning mountain in Jer. li, 25. "Wormwood" (viii, 11) occurs in Jer. ix, 15, and Amos v, 7. The darkening of the heavenly bodies (viii, 12) is found also in Isa. xiii, 10; Amos viii, 9; and Joel ii, 31. "Locusts" (ix, 3) are mentioned in Exod. x, 4; Nahum iii, 17; Joel i, 4.

But the assemblage of the events in the Revelation differs from any other in the Bible. It is more systematically arranged than in the series foretold by our Lord in Matt. xxiv. It differs from the account of the Egyptian plagues of Exodus in omissions, the introduction of new details, and

Means by which Advanced

in the fact that the plagues occur in a different order. The hail, for instance, which is the seventh Egyptian plague, is the first of the plagues in the Revelation. All this may be explained by the fact that the plagues of Egypt were confined to that country and were adapted to its local climatic conditions, while the plagues of the Revelation have for their field the world itself, and were intentionally diversified in being fitted to this larger sphere.

That a close connection exists between man and his dwelling place, the earth, is a truth in which both science and the Scriptures cordially concur; the dispute, if any, between them is not as to the fact, but its cause. The doctrine of evolution, which receives such wide acceptance, rests upon this connection as a fundamental axiom; and the Scriptures confirm the fact in the accounts of the creation and the fall. The difference between science and the Scriptures is, that what evolution attributes to the operation of natural law the Bible explains by the working of a moral power. As for man's sake the ground was cursed and all nature made to suffer by reason of his rebellion, so do they bear constant witness to his advance or degeneration in righteousness. As purity is in general promotive of prosperity, so does sin produce disaster. "As the moral life of the soul expresses itself in the physical life of the body for the latter's health or corruption, so the conduct of the human race affects the physical life of the universe to its farthest limit in space. The Old Testament is not contented with a general statement of this great principle, but pursues it to all sorts of particular and private applications. The curses of the Lord fell, not only on the sinner, but on his dwelling, his property, and even on the bit of ground he occupied. The doctrine of the Old Testament is that man's sin has rendered necessary the destruction of his material circumstances, and that the divine judgment includes a broken and rifled universe." *

And these calamities, whether brought about directly by the divine Governor, or through the operation of general laws, which is but another mode of his action, are so many trumpet calls from God warning men to retrace their erring steps and submit to his

---

* *Isaiah*, vol. i. chap. xxxviii, pp. 419, ff., in the *Expositor's Bible*, New York, A. C. Armstrong & Co.

kingdom. "It was plague and fire," Leigh Hunt says, "that first taught the Londoners to build their city better." And the divine Being may make use of like means to forward his moral government.

1. *Natural Providences.*—In the *first* trumpet scene the blow falls upon the earth itself. Its productive resources were severely diminished through the destructive agencies of nature, intensified, it may be, by the horrors of war. The hail and the fire were mingled with blood. And, since food is essential to life, "the king himself being served by the field," such a disaster must sorely oppress mankind. The apostle had himself witnessed at least one widely-extended famine, and had noted how the exhibition of Christian benevolence had been made the means of promoting the kingdom of Christ (Acts xi, 28-30).

The *second* trumpet scene deals with disasters affecting "the sea," the great highway of commerce, and disturbing the exchanges of the products of labor among men. More than once in the history of the world social revolutions have been the plowshare turning up the soil, that seeds of religious reformation might the better grow.

In the *third* trumpet scene it is the sources of water supply that are affected. A star, falling from heaven, turns them to wormwood, which in the Old Testament is used as a symbol of bitterness and poisoning. It is in the contamination of these sources that epidemics and pestilences usually find their commencement, and a merciful Providence generally spares them until other and milder warnings have been tried.

In the *fourth* trumpet scene the heavenly bodies are involved, carrying out the idea, so frequently expressed in the Bible, of the sympathy which the whole creation seems to feel with the great events transacted on earth. The universe is so bound together that whatever touches one part of the great Governor's empire ultimately affects every other (Exod. x, 21–24; Isa. xiii, 9–11; Joel ii, 31; Matt. xxiv, 29; xxvii, 45). Yet the images in this scene may be figurative emblems of the ruling powers of earthly kingdoms, and the vision may be interpreted as synonymous with the predictions of Hag. ii, 6–9, and Heb. xii, 26–29, in which the shaking of heaven and earth is made to precede the coming of the kingdom of Christ.

Means by which Advanced

The *fifth* trumpet scene is undoubtedly the most difficult of all to interpret and requires more elaborate treatment. In striving to explain its obscurities the only safe and satisfactory method is to search for what may be regarded as certain and plain in the vision, and from this as a starting point to essay the more difficult.

Two things seem to stand out prominently and comparatively clearly in the scene. Assuming the star which fell from heaven, to whom was given the key of the bottomless pit, and who is closely connected with the angel of the pit named Abaddon or Apollyon—that is, destroyer—to be a representation of Satan, then for the first time this archenemy of God and man is introduced personally upon the stage. In whatever the fifth trumpet signifies he directly or indirectly has a preëminent share. Then, again, the mention of locusts points us to the prophecy of Joel, where the destructive ravages of this scourge are such a conspicuous figure. If we can reach a satisfactory solution of Joel's prophecy we may reasonably expect an understanding of this prophecy of the Revelation.

In the great prophecy of Joel, brief in

extent, but comprehensive in import, the background upon which the earnest preacher of God paints his vivid pictures is the alarming condition of spiritual declension and apathy into which the people had fallen, accompanied with fearful neglect of the service of God and its ordinances. To awaken the people out of this deadly state he predicts the approach of an awful scourge, the ravages of which would be felt in a resultant condition of extraordinary impoverishment and penury. Poverty of spirit must precede entrance into the riches of the kingdom of heaven. And so the prophet is commissioned to promise that, after repentance and renewal of consecration, there shall be a rich and plentiful effusion of the Holy Spirit; and he assures the penitent that "whosoever shall call on the name of the Lord shall be delivered" and shall escape the impending destruction.

Nothing is more probable, therefore, than that the writer of the Revelation meant to warn the Church of Christ against a decline in faith or relaxation in zeal. He assured it that such a lapse would be followed by the intrusion into its field of some dangerous enemy. What the character of this enemy should be is indicated by two things. It will be noticed that, if John deviates from the description of the locusts given by Joel, it is in the direction of bringing humanity more into the picture. The locusts spoken of in this fifth trumpet scene are to have crowns like gold upon their heads; their faces are to be as the faces of men; their hair to be as the hair of women; they are to hurt, not as real locusts do, the earth and its products, but men; their sting, unlike that of other locusts, is to be as the sting of scorpions; and their work will be, not the destruction of human life, but the causing of such misery as to make human life unhappy and undesirable. They are to be under the direction of Satan, whose field of operations in the warfare he wages against the kingdom of Christ is, not the earth, but the world of human beings.

The truth, then, which seems to be indicated in this obscure vision is, that whenever a Christian man or Church declines into lukewarmness or apathy there may be expected to follow an incursion and invasion by other and lower forms of religious life and thought. Wherever iniquity abounds and the "love of many" waxes cold there is sure to be an inroad of heresy, false doctrine, more or less heterodoxy of creed. The human heart, like nature, abhors a vacuum. Where true godliness wanes false religions rush in to fill the void; and the intensity of zeal which false religions awaken measures the declension that has befallen true faith. The evil spirit that comes back to a home from which he has been once expelled, and finds it empty, swept, and garnished, takes to himself seven other spirits more wicked than himself, "and the last state of that man is worse than the first." The temperature of religion when it falls to lower levels never does so equably. The nobler and more ideal parts suffer most severely, and, like the shriveled idol of the Philistines, at last "only the stump of Dagon is left to him."

There can be no question that the advocates of the historical interpretation of the Revelation have a very strong support for their hypothesis in the application of this part of it to the rise and growth of Mohammedanism. It is not to be denied that many of the essential characteristics of that false religion are quite accurately delineated in this picture. The rise and rapid extension of Mohammedanism were possible only because of the dead, formal, and corrupt condition of the Christendom which it encountered. Its prophet and founder preached a faith which was purer than that of many a so-called Christian bishop; and it achieves its triumphs now only in those regions where Christianity has degenerated into spiritual barrenness and puerile ceremonialism. But in this, as in so many instances, the historical interpretation errs, not through incorrectness, so much as through incompleteness. In claiming any one historical event as the fulfillment of prophecy it impoverishes inspiration by confining that fulfillment to a single fact. Mohammedanism is but one illustration of a profounder truth. The Revelation of John is meant for all ages. It is constantly finding new illustrations and applications. In setting before us the causes of decline as well as of growth, the Revelation teaches us to be looking for these causes at all times, that we may avert the decline or forward the growth; and thus it is furnishing new examples of its divine truth and new evidences of its divine origin, without exhausting its force in any single example or any single evidence.

The *sixth* trumpet sounds, and the vision which is presented to us is one of increasing danger and darkness. Warnings unheeded give way to alarms still more threatening. The noonday bell of invitation deepens into the curfew toll of departing day. The approach of an immense and imposing array of horsemen armed for battle strikes deeper terror than did the invasion of the locusts and indicates judgments more formidable. The power of Satan to harm is overmastering mercy's efforts to save, and the restrictions which had been laid upon his authority are being relaxed. We are told now that "by these three was the third part of men killed, by the fire, and by the smoke, and by the brimstone." As there is suggested a spiritual condition which has gone beyond mere declension and apathy to deeper states of alienation from God, so the perils threatened end, not with a destruction of the happiness of life, but in death itself.

It must be noticed that the region from which the new and alarming scourge proceeds is the "great river Euphrates." To understand this we must place ourselves at

Means by which Advanced

the standpoint of the apostle. The river Euphrates was to Palestine what the Danube and the Rhine were to the Roman empire—the line of demarcation between civilization and barbarism. The East was the quarter from which the earlier prophets always apprehended danger. It was in the Euphrates that Jeremiah was bidden to cast the book with the stone tied to it (Jer. li, 63). On the hither side of the great river lay the kingdoms with which Israel had mainly had intercourse. On the north of Palestine was Syria, on the south, Egypt; on the banks of the Euphrates and Tigris or near by were Assyria and Babylon. The peoples of these kingdoms were, indeed, nations whose God was not the Lord; yet between them and Israel a *modus vivendi* had to some degree been established, and some common rules of international intercourse were recognized. But on the farther side was the land of barbarians among whom the arts of civilization were unknown, who acknowledged no code of comity or obligation with which the chosen people were familiar, whose ways and modes of warfare were impenetrable and strange, and from whom all possible evils might be expected.

There is, it must be sadly confessed, in all human beings a latent germ of barbarism, a survival of the carnal or animal nature. Suppressed, indeed, it may be by culture, education, or other moral or secular forces, and its existence hardly surmised, yet it only awaits fostering conditions to manifest its presence and reassert its power. Without divine grace no Christian is free from liability to an outburst of the carnal mind which may destroy the spiritual life of the soul. Nor does any grade of civilization exempt nations from the possibility of a reversion to barbarism, if the excitements to it are allowed to exist or precautions against its inroads are neglected. Bishop Butler expressed the opinion that whole communities, like individuals, might become insane. Perhaps it is nearer the truth to explain the sudden frenzies to which men and nations have sometimes given way as an uncontrolled irruption of the barbarous element within. Farther on, in the twentieth chapter of the Revelation, we shall find this tendency toward barbarism more particularly referred to by John, and the appreciation of it will help us there to solve one of the most perplexing problems of the book.

Means by which Advanced

Ethnology either ignores this liability to revert to barbarism or denies it, and by so doing impairs the value of those hypotheses as to the primitive condition of the race which it seeks to substitute for the Bible story. It is not always easy to determine whether any particular stage of barbarism marks a step upward in the advance of a growing people or a decline toward animalism from a superior state; yet the correctness of our inferences depends upon an accurate diagnosis of this question.

But human experience is constantly furnishing illustrations confirming the utterances of the word of God as to the possibility of a fall from high grades of cultivation to the depths of savagery. If the counsels of God are unheeded and the convictions of the Holy Spirit are resisted nothing can follow but a descent into lower grades, until the savage forces that underlie our nature assert supremacy and overleap the weak barriers which reason and judgment set up to stay them.

Something like this seems to be the warning meant to be conveyed through the sixth trumpet. A striking commentary upon this was given but a few centuries after John's death, when the hordes of barbarians that had been only waiting opportunity swept with irresistible fury over the crumbling walls of the corrupt and decadent Roman Empire, and imposed upon the Christian Church the task of saving civilization itself from destruction. We may not even now relax our watchfulness or put off the armor of our faith, lest this may involve a reversion of mankind to barbaric naturalism. And a return to barbarism is the lowest condition to which human nature can fall. From such a state recovery is well-nigh hopeless and repentance an extreme improbability, for the resources of mercy will have been almost exhausted, and beyond lies only doom.

It should be noticed that the Revelation speaks of three woes. The first one predicted is described under the fifth trumpet. The second one is declared by the sixth trumpet. The third one is not uncovered at all. It lies in that future world from which the curtain is not lifted and into which even the light of revelation feebly penetrates. Whoever has rejected all the warnings of love and descended the moral scale until he has reverted to the state of sensualism is but a step from the second death. "He that soweth to his flesh shall of the flesh reap corruption."

2. *The Two Witnesses, or, the Supernatural Scriptures.*—The episode of the "two witnesses," to which we are now brought, is one that has sorely tried expositors. Though many and various solutions of it have been attempted, Alford, in his commentary upon the passage, says, "I will further remark, and the reader will find this abundantly borne out by research into histories of Apocalyptic exegesis, that no solution at all approaching to a satisfactory one has ever yet been given . . . of this portion of the prophecy." If it shall be found, therefore, that the principles which have hitherto guided us enable us to penetrate to the core of this mystery, and evolve a meaning intelligible and reasonable, and which, while interpreting all the details without distortion or suppression, is in harmony at the same time with the Scriptures in general and with the purpose for which they have been revealed, then we may indulge the hope that these principles are correct and may advance with some confidence to the

problems that still lie before us. Though long tunnels are yet to be threaded, with only brief intervals between them of open air, we shall in time, perhaps, reach the light of day and rest in the sunshine of discovered truth.

It has been already said that through the vast space that intervenes between the divine Being and man two great lines of communication stretch. These are his works and his word. It is this truth which the trumpets symbolize, and we have not yet gotten beyond the section of the Revelation in which this emblem of the trumpets is the ruling one. Six of the trumpets have sounded. Whatever can be done by natural providences to arouse men to spiritual thought and action has been sounded by them. Nature has no other voices with which to speak to mankind. But the resources of Omnipotence are not exhausted. God has yet other means of approach to his creatures. And if, therefore, because of heedlessness or obduracy or preoccupation of mind or absorption in temporal things, one of these lines of light from God's mercy falls with too light a touch to arrest men's attention or awaken them to danger or win

Means by which Advanced

their consent to seek God's favor, there remains another and more efficient one, namely, his written word; and here is the place where we should expect allusion to it.

The two witnesses, then, may be reasonably interpreted as signifying the *law* and the *prophets*, the titles under which the Old Testament Scriptures received by John as divinely inspired were almost universally designated. Should these fail of their purpose, even the divine Being, we may reverently say, had no other way of reaching man. It is our Lord himself who says, " If they hear not Moses and the prophets, neither will they be persuaded though one rose from the dead." When the great and strong wind rending the mountains, and after this the earthquake, and after this the fire, have failed, it is possible that the still small voice will arouse to faith and hope and duty. Should it not do so, then the case is hopeless.

In order to verify the solution which is here proposed of the episode of the two witnesses, a careful examination will be made of the facts as detailed in the text.

The introduction of the two witnesses, however, is preceded by two visions by way of prelude. This, we shall find, is what we might reasonably expect. If the witnesses are, indeed, symbols of the sacred Scriptures, God's direct revelation of his will and character to men, it is proper that the scope and purpose of all revelation shall be plainly laid down, that we may know how far the revealed word of God is to be regarded as evidence, and also that some criteria shall be given by which we shall be able to discern what the inspired writings are, and how to differentiate them from human productions. In other words, we have here from the pen of John his own views of biblical criticism, and it would have been well if they had been more carefully heeded in the discussions of inspiration recently so rife.

In the first of these two visions a "mighty angel" is seen to "come down from heaven, clothed with a cloud" and with "a rainbow upon his head." And he had in his hand a little book open. But, when "seven thunders had uttered their voices" and John was "about to write," a voice was heard from heaven saying, "Seal up those things which the seven thunders uttered, and write them not." This prohibition is distinctly declared to be only for a time. " In the days of the voice of the seventh angel, when he shall begin to sound, the mystery of God should be finished, as he hath declared unto his servants the prophets."

If the interpretation put upon the two witnesses is correct, and if they symbolize the Scriptures, then the purpose of this prelude is to indicate what we are to look for in them. It is not the design of the Bible to communicate all possible truth, but only such measure of it as has reference to the kingdom of Christ. Although the things which are revealed belong to us and to our children, there are still secret things which belong to the Lord our God. He has communicated much, but he has withheld much, and doubtless the reasons for the revelation and the reserve are equally wise. There are truths which man's own powers enable him to discover. There are other truths beyond his ability to comprehend even should they be revealed. These are excluded from the Scriptures as being aside from their purpose. It is only "when that which is perfect is come," and "that which is in part shall be done away," that we shall know as we are known. Very much that we know not now we shall know hereafter. But the

Bible has specific reference to the kingdom of Christ and reveals only what has relation to that kingdom. "The testimony of Jesus" is the spirit of all prophecy. That which lies within the capacity of man to discover is left to the wisdom and patience of men. That which pertains to the future life, and would simply satisfy curiosity to know, is reserved to the time when we shall have laid aside mortality. The Scriptures reveal to us only what it is needful for us to know that we may enter and enjoy and forward the kingom of Christ. Paul was not allowed to utter the words he had heard in his heavenly ecstasy, and John is likewise prohibited from uttering things which belong solely to the divine Being and await his pleasure to publish. It was sufficient for him to be told that, however bitter and unpalatable his message might be, he must still "prophesy before many peoples, and nations, and tongues, and kings."

The second prelude also has reference to the limitations within which all revelation is confined. "There was given me a reed like unto a rod: and the angel stood, saying, Rise, and measure the temple of God, and the altar, and them that worship therein. But the court which is without the temple leave out, and measure it not; for it is given unto the Gentiles: and the holy city shall they tread under foot forty and two months."

There are two elements in this which furnish guides to its interpretation. One is the distinction so emphatically made between the temple itself, which, as we know, was reserved exclusively for Israelites, and the outer courts, which were given to the Gentiles. The other is the use of the symbolical number forty-two.

Now is it not a reasonable thing that the apostle, when about to point us to the law and the prophets as God's two witnesses, shall put a broad distinction between them and all mere human productions? The temple itself is the field within which they fulfill their office, and those only who speak from it are God's accredited messengers. If the Scriptures are the standard by which truth concerning the kingdom of Christ is to be tested, if they have authority to bind the consciences of men, there must be some criterion by which they shall be judged. And this is the criterion—"Salvation is of the Jews." God's messengers and witnesses sprang from them. And Paul confirms this declaration when he says that the chief advantage which the Jews had was that "unto them were committed the oracles of God." The highest creations of human genius fall short of the special inspiration which belonged to the prophets and patriarchs and apostles of Israel. The outer courts, indeed, were given to the Gentiles. Theirs was the world of art, of science, of commerce, of literature, of politics, of earthly dominion; but the temple and the altar belonged to the chosen race. Brilliant stars brightened the darkness of the Gentile sky, but the sun of spiritual truth shone only to the teachers whom God called out of Israel; and Homer and Æschylus, and muse and sibyl, must "pale their ineffectual fires" in the presence of his seers and anointed ones. And this is confirmed by the use of the symbolical number forty-two. This number, as we have seen in the Introduction, typifies a period which has definite limits and fulfills a specific purpose. It may designate Judaism proper or Gentilism proper. And the meaning here is that now, and throughout this present cycle of time, the kingdom of God has been taken from the Jew and given to a nation bringing forth the fruits of the kingdom. Neither the temple, nor the altar, nor the inspired Scriptures belong now exclusively to the Jew. The chosen race has forfeited its prerogative of exclusiveness, and the foot of the Gentile treads the inner as well as outer court. The Bible belongs to us as well as to Israel.

With these important and interesting preludes explained, and the reason of their introduction in this place accounted for, we are prepared to investigate the vision of the two witnesses.

It has already been said, but the importance of the matter requires its repetition, that the paragraph containing the vision of the witnesses is a part of the section of the Revelation of which the trumpet is the ruling symbol; for it is not until the close of this paragraph that the seventh trumpet sounds. It seems, therefore, plausible that what is symbolized by the witnesses has some continuous connection with that which is designated by the trumpets. And, inasmuch as the trumpets are emblems of the instrumentalities which the divine Being employs to call men to repentance, obedience, and the service of himself, the witnesses are an emblem of some such instrumentality, having the same end in view, but operating in a different mode. The six trumpets which have already sounded represent what the divine Being does by way of natural providence, approaching men by calamities, distresses, the observed connection between impiety and moral, as well as intellectual, decadence, and such like means. But nature in any and all of its modes of manifestation does not comprise all the modes of communication between God and man. Nor is the testimony which it bears to God the highest testimony. The same Being who "formeth the mountains, and createth the wind," who "maketh the morning darkness, and treadeth upon the high places of the earth," also "declareth unto man what is his thought." "The heavens," indeed, "declare the glory of God; and the firmament showeth his handiwork." But the law of God does more. It converteth the soul. Nature's witness is given by dumb signs or inarticulate sounds. It has no speech nor language. Its worshipers may cry aloud to their Baal from morning until the time of the evening sacrifice, but there is none to hear, nor any God that regards. It is to and through the human spirit that the divine Spirit must communicate his deepest truths; nor has he done all that may be done until he has given to men his word. "The grass withereth, the flower fadeth; but the word of our God shall stand forever."

The two witnesses, human and intelligent, aptly and appropriately represent this higher mode of communication which God employs to impress and teach men. By them we are to understand the law and the prophets, the two component parts of the Old Testament Scriptures, which at the date of the Apocalypse constituted the only canonical Scriptures known. In the paragraph which follows there is an intimation of the New Testament; but as yet it was not in existence as a collected code. The Bible which Christ and his apostles knew was the Jewish Bible.

The proof of this somewhat novel interpretation of the two witnesses, if, indeed, any interpretation of any part of the Apocalypse can be called novel, lies in the fact that it explains all the details of the vision which are presented to us simply, easily, and without any forced construction. It is essential to group together the separate details, and then endeavor to explain them.

The seer says of these two witnesses that they prophesy in sackcloth twelve hundred and sixty days, which, as has been said in discussing rules of interpretation, is one of the numbers symbolical of Judaism; they are identified as corresponding with the "two sons of oil, that stand by the Lord of the whole earth," of whom Zechariah wrote (Revised Version); they have power to devour their enemies and shut heaven by the miracles of withholding the rain, turning waters to blood, and smiting the earth with plagues. There is a period when their "testimony" is finished. When that period is reached their enemy, the beast from the bottomless pit, kills them, and their dead bodies lie exposed for three and a half days "in the street of the great city, which spiritually is called Sodom and Egypt, where also our Lord was crucified." At the end of this period "the Spirit of life entered into them, and they stood upon their feet;" and they finally "ascended up to heaven" amid convulsions which shake the earth and fill men with terror.

How accurately all these features of the paragraph find their fulfillment in the law and the prophets, or the Old Testament Scriptures, may be readily shown:

First. It is worthy of consideration as a strong point that the expression, "the law and the prophets" (sometimes "Moses and the prophets"), is the one almost invariably employed by our Lord in designating the older Scriptures (Matt. v, 17; vii, 12; xi, 13; xxii, 40; Luke xvi, 31; xxiv, 27; as also John i, 45; Acts xiii, 15; xxviii, 23).

Secondly. The testimony of the prophets and writers of the Old Testament may be truly said to have been given in sackcloth. What one of these messengers of God ever met with a cordial reception? Well did Stephen say, perhaps in the hearing of John himself, "Which of the prophets have not your fathers persecuted?" "They were stoned, were sawn asunder, were tempted, were slain with the sword: they wandered about in sheepskins, and goatskins; being destitute, afflicted, tormented" (Heb. xi, 37; Luke, xi, 49–51).

Thirdly. The law and the prophets found their special embodiments and representatives in Moses (John i, 17) and Elijah (Mal.

iv, 4, 5); one the unequaled statesmen and legislator, the other the most striking and, in many respects, the greatest of the long line of prophets. The miracles ascribed to the two witnesses were actually wrought by these two extraordinary and typical men. To Moses was given power to turn waters to blood and to smite the earth with plagues. It was at the prayer of Elijah that the heaven was shut so that it rained not but according to his word.

Fourthly. Zechariah's vision of the "two olive branches which through the two golden pipes empty the golden oil out of themselves," and which are said to be "the two anointed ones, that stand by the Lord of the whole earth," finds its most appropriate and exact fulfillment in the Holy Scriptures, which testify of Jesus (John v, 39). And it was the representatives of the law and the prophets, or Moses and Elijah, who were chosen to stand by our Lord when he appeared in glory upon the Mount of Transfiguration.

Fifthly. The "testimony" of the law and the prophets is distinctly said by our Lord himself to have been "finished" when his own forerunner, John the Baptist, appeared.

"For all the prophets and the law prophesied until John" (Matt. xi, 13); "The law and the prophets were until John" (Luke xvi, 16).

Sixthly. Although the Jews professedly acknowledged the law and the prophets to be of divine origin, our Lord emphatically charged against them that they had by their glosses and traditions in effect abrogated them; devitalizing them and making their authority to be a dead letter (Matt. xv, 6; Mark vii, 13; Luke xi, 52).

Seventhly. At no period did this nullification of the power of the Holy Scriptures reach such extremes as during our Lord's active ministry on earth. The dead bodies of the law and the prophets may be said, without exaggeration, to have lain exposed in the streets of Jerusalem, where our Lord was crucified.

Eighthly. The bodies of the two witnesses are said to have lain "three days and a half." As the period of our Lord's active ministry has been computed at three and a half years the number may refer to that. But as three and a half is a symbolical number, designating a half period, it may be used to designate the same here. The ministry of our Lord was such a half period, which was not completed until it had been supplemented by the gift of the Holy Spirit.

Ninthly. After the " three days and a half the Spirit of life from God " is said to have " entered into " the two witnesses, " and they stood upon their feet." This was remarkably fulfilled on the day of Pentecost, when, by the illumination and inspiration of the Holy Ghost, the apostles were moved to draw from the law and the prophets those convincing arguments and promises and appeals which led to the conversion of thousands.

Tenthly. The two witnesses after their resurrection are said to have " ascended up to heaven " in the presence of their enemies. This finds its fulfillment in the fact that the Hebrew Scriptures, with the added life given them by the New Testament, have been accepted by the Christian Church, not as the exclusive property of the Jewish Church or as the archives of the Hebrew nation, but as the common heritage of the world and the canonical word of God to the whole human race.

Lastly. The convulsions of nature which are said to have accompanied the ascent of the witnesses to heaven were exactly fulfilled, as John could testify, in the events that followed Pentecost—the terror and alarm of Christ's enemies, the fear that came upon all, the shaking as by an earthquake of the place where the disciples were assembled in prayer, and the rapid increase in numbers of those who were slain of the Lord and raised to a new spiritual life.

If this explanation of the episode of the two witnesses is correct the depreciation, or rather, perhaps, under-appreciation of the Old Testament, which exists even among those who do not question its inspiration, is without ground or reason. In the opinion of St. John the addition of the New Testament does not in any wise supersede or render obsolete the older Scriptures. In the education of the human race the Creator did not begin with the more abstruse and highly developed teachings of the New Testament, but with the natural, biographical, historical, and providential facts of the Old. With the exception of the evangelical gospels, which belong really to both dispensations, since the Christ whose life and words and deeds are there recorded is both the consummation of the one dispensation and the seed and promise of the other, no part of holy writ exceeds in interest, attractiveness, and simplicity the law and the prophets, in which John and Peter and Paul were trained.

The Old Testament contains, albeit in embryo, all doctrines and truths essential to the kingdom of Christ. If for a while it was kept secreted within the bounds of Judaism, this was not because its revelations were meant exclusively for the chosen people, but that its sacred treasures might be guarded from waste and wanton destruction until the rest of the world was prepared to welcome them. If much of its meaning was misconceived and misconstrued by the Jewish mind, this must be attributed largely to the frailty and ignorance of human nature. The New Testament does not so much add to the Old Testament as illustrate, explain, and apply it. It is the interpreter, not the destroyer, of the Old. It opens its secrets, brings to light its truths, reveals to us the face of Jesus Christ everywhere in it, and enforces its teachings by the power of the Holy Spirit. But the Scriptures of the Old Testament are the imperishable record of the foundation of

Means by which Advanced

Christ's kingdom upon earth. Without them the writings of the New Testament would be without connection with that continuous chain of inspiration whose first link was forged when God said, "Let there be light." And, equally so, without the New Testament the Old would be merely a foundation lacking a superstructure, and thus incomplete. Its chain of inspiration would be without any sure anchorage in the future eternity, and thus hang helpless and useless, with no power to bridge the gulf between the alpha and omega, the beginning of time and its end. But the Old Testament can never become obsolete. Not one jot or tittle of it shall pass away until all is fulfilled. And the revelation given in the New Testameut can no more supersede or abolish it than science can supersede nature, of which it is the ordained expositor.

There is a healthiness, too, about the Old Testament like to the quiet restfulness of nature. When men are disposed to wander from the safe path into the vagaries of mysticism or asceticism nothing will correct the aberrance more surely than diligent and profound study of its sober realities and its everyday life. The reading of it calms the fevers and dispels the illusions to which we are prone. It brings to us those soothing influences which we feel when we look at the

> "Good gigantic smile of the brown old earth
> On autumn mornings,"

or, lying under forest shades, watch the gentle swaying of foliage, or listen to the purling of brooks, or catch glimpses of the calm blue sky. We need its concrete facts to save us from the abstractions of a vague and unreal idealism.

Thus closes the vision of the trumpets. They represent the messengers whom God employs to call men to repentance, the methods he avails himself of to forward the kingdom within and without us. He will not cease to strive with us until every appeal likely to reach us has been tried. When nature and the supernatural, the word of God in providence and the richer word of God in revelation, have exerted their power the resources of the divine Being have been, we may with all reverence say, exhausted, and the time is ripe for the closing of the drama of probation, that he which is righteous may be righteous still, and he which is filthy may be filthy still.

Means by which Advanced

Yet the writer of the Revelation does not allow us to remain in doubt as to the result of God's efforts to save a lost world. The wisdom of God is not astray. "He will rest in his love." He has himself absolute confidence in the success of the plans of redemption. When the *seventh* and last trumpet shall sound the curtain will fall upon a world restored to God, upon a paradise regained, and great voices in heaven shall say, "The kingdoms of this world are become the kingdoms of our Lord, and of his Christ; and he shall reign forever and ever."

PART IV
The Foes of the Kingdom

PART IV
The Foes of the Kingdom

WITH chapter xii another section of the Apocalypse begins. Two great truths relating to the kingdom of Christ have been discussed—the fundamental principle of mediatorial sovereignty upon which it is based, and the instruments, providence and the written word, by which it is advanced. It follows very naturally and logically that the antagonists by whom the kingdom is opposed should also be disclosed to us. Out of his abundant grace and in tender compassion for human ignorance, God has made known to us, through this marvelous book, the adversaries with whom we must contend before the kingdom can attain its consummation in our hearts or in the world at large.

While no part of the Revelation is easy of interpretation, or can be made intelligible without very careful study both of itself and of the whole Bible, there has been added to this part of it the embarrassment of the *odium theologicum*. Bitter controversial strifes have raged around the interpretation of it and have raised a cloud of prejudices, through which the truth has been sometimes dimly seen. From all such prejudices we must free ourselves. We are approaching holy ground, and it behooves us to put off our shoes, that nothing of human invention may intervene between our naked feet and the sacred floor of God's temple.

We need this caution the more because from the nature of the case the interpretation of this part carries us more or less into the field of history. The foes of the kingdom of Christ are visible foes, as well as invisible. The contest is not only for the individual man, but for the race. The commission given to the Church is, "Go, preach my Gospel to every creature;" and the keynote of the song of triumph with which the last part closed was, "The kingdoms of this world are become the kingdoms of our Lord, and of his Christ."

There is, therefore, a tendency to confine the interpretation to the field of history, to direct the attention to large and collective bodies of men, either world powers or religious societies, or to those historical events and cycles of events which have apparently changed the currents of the ages, and to insist that in these the fulfillment of the prophecy lies.

But history itself is only the record of individuals. We delude ourselves when we fancy that by association anything is created. That mystical something which is imagined to be in collective bodies more than in the individuals that compose them is a mere figment of the brain, and to discuss it is simply to revive the barren conceits of the schoolmen. A Church is only "a congregation of believing men;" a State is a coöperative association of individuals, not a corporation; and neither one has any powers or forces other than those which exist in the individual members. Man is both the microcosm and the macrocosm.

The chief value of the inspired book which we are now studying lies in the fact that it discloses to us those forces, spiritual and otherwise, the conflict between which makes up the life history of each individual of mankind. It is a chart meant for every navigator of this boundless ocean of human existence. Its truths will be as precious and important to the last man on this globe as they are to us. The reefs and breakers it describes are not perils past which any age can sail and then look back upon as things done with, but dangers which beset every voyager. It is true that in the history of large bodies of men, whether secular or religious in their character—in the temptations, declension, growth, and triumph of nations and Churches—illustrations of its truths and fulfillments of its predictions will be found. But these, we must insist, are merely illustrations. Long as the world shall last the Apocalyse will prove itself to be a part of God's boon of revelation, in that each follower of Christ shall find it of inestimable value for his own private guidance, inspiration, and study.

Looking by the light of God's lamp through the ages to come, John was allowed to foresee the successful completion of the lifework and plans of Jesus the Saviour. He who began both his gospel and his great epistle with "the beginning" also follows the course of the drama of redemption to its final "amen." The saint who, leaning on the bosom of Jesus, looked up to him as the Author of his faith was also permitted to fall at his majestic feet and worship him as its Finisher. And, from personal com-

The Foes of the Kingdom

munion with and contemplation of him as the Son of man, he rose to the grander conception of him as the Christ, the Word of God, King of kings, and Lord of lords. He was taught, also, that the progress through which his own conceptions of the Son of God had passed was but a type and example of that which shall take place in time on the field of the world and in the hearts of mankind. The cross upon which Jesus of Nazareth suffered was, indeed, a throne from which he ascended to the crown of the universe. But John, too, saw that ere that final consummation can be reached there are foes to be encountered, hindrances to be removed, antagonists to be overthrown. A great and effectual door is opened unto us, but there are many adversaries. To the consideration of these he therefore now calls our attention:

1. *The Dragon, or Satan.*—The first of the adversaries with whom the kingdom of Christ has to dispute supremacy is the devil, the archfiend and enemy of God and man.

That Satan, the evil one, is referred to in the description of the great red dragon having seven heads, ten horns, and seven diadems seems an interpretation so natural that it is hardly worth while to seek for farfetched meanings when so plausible an explanation lies near at hand. The ten horns (Zechariah saw but four—Zech. i, 18) are the instruments with which he seeks to scatter and destroy the sheep of God. The seven heads with diadems represent the pride and haughtiness of spirit in which he boasts that the power and glory of all kingdoms have been delivered to him and that he gives them to whom he will. It is a struggle for life and death between him and the Christ. If Paul, the man of affairs, with his practical conception of things in their concrete relations, says, "Our wrestling is not against flesh and blood, but against the principalities, against the powers, against the world-rulers of this darkness, against the spiritual hosts of wickedness in the heavenly places" (Revised Version), much more strongly does John, with his intuition of abstract principles, recognize and emphasize the power and working of the dark spirit whose names are Satan and "destroyer." No writer of the New Testament speaks oftener or more clearly of the evil spirit than does John. In vivid imagery and with graphic condensation he sums up

The Foes of the Kingdom

the history of the kingdom of darkness, the long record of Satan's undying antagonism to the kingdom of Christ.

The woman arrayed "with the sun, and the moon under her feet, and upon her head a crown of twelve stars" (see Gen. xxxvii, 9), represents the Church collectively and in its most general expression; primarily, the Jewish Church, inasmuch as Christianity had just begun its mission; but not confined thereto. Against the Church, against every individual of it, this murderer and liar from the beginning wages relentless warfare. His is the power behind all other antagonisms. To devour the child of the woman in the hour of its birth, to destroy humanity itself if he can, seems to be the aim of his being. Not a soul is now born into the kingdom of Christ by regenerating grace but Satan is there to crush the newly-given life, if possible, in its inception.

When the first gospel of salvation and victory was given to Eve, "Thy seed shall bruise the serpent's head," Satan began his machinations to defeat the prophecy, even though he knew that he could do no more than bruise the heel of the promised seed.

When the promise given to Abraham of a posterity countless as the stars of heaven was about to receive its fulfillment in the extraordinary fertility of the sons of Jacob in Egypt, it was Satan who inspired Pharaoh to issue the cruel edict commanding the death of every Hebrew male child.

When Jesus was born in Bethlehem of Judea it was the same dragon that urged Herod to his mad purpose of slaying every young child throughout its coasts. "This is the heir ; let us kill him, that the inheritance may be ours."

And it is against this wily foe, "the prince of the power of the air," "the spirit that now worketh in the children of disobedience," that we all have continually to struggle.

For protection against such an adversary there is certainly need of divine aid. And that help has never been withheld. "There were given to the woman the two wings of a great eagle." Is not this an echo of Exod. xix, 4, "I bare you on eagles' wings," and also of Psalm xci, 4, "And under his wings shalt thou trust"? And in addition to this we are told that God prepared "a place" in the wilderness where the woman might fly and be nourished. Does not this refer to

The Foes of the Kingdom

Palestine, that quiet, secluded land, nigh the great highways of the world and yet aloof from them, where in comparative isolation Israel might develop her own resources and grow in strength until she should be ready for her broader mission ? If the purpose of the divine Being fell short of full realization the fault was not his, but hers, through her lust to be like the surrounding nations.

The numbers, too, representing the period of this seclusion, "twelve hundred and sixty days," and "a time, times, and half a time," are forms of three and a half, which, as has been said in the Introduction, symbolizes Judaism, or any cycle with a definite purpose which is, however, only a half period.

And further confirmation of the reference to the Church of Israel is found in the allusion to the archangel Michael, who is always represented in the Scriptures as sustaining some special relation to Israel (Dan. x, 21; xii, 1).

Yet, mighty as Satan is and venomous as is his hostility, the believer is endowed with weapons of offense and defense still more potent. "They overcame him by the blood of the Lamb, and by the word of their testimony" (or "witness" with reference, doubtless, to the testimony of the two witnesses of the preceding chapter). In other words, the cross of Christ and the word of God are the conquering weapons with which believers win the victory over Satan. The Lord Jesus had most plainly foretold the secret of victory in the hearing of John when he had said, "Now is the judgment of this world: now shall the prince of this world be cast out. And I, if I be lifted up from the earth, will draw all men unto me." And, doubtless, these words came with fullness and force to the memory of the apostle when he heard the "loud voice saying in heaven, Now is come salvation and strength, and the kingdom of our God, and the power of his Christ: for the accuser of our brethren is cast down."

Not yet, however, is Satan ready to cease his efforts to destroy. He changes the field of conflict, but does not relinquish the malice of his assault. If he cannot in heaven, that is, the Church, countervail the kingdom of Christ, he will attempt it in the earth, on the field of secular life. "The serpent cast out of his mouth water as a flood, after the woman: that he might

The Foes of the Kingdom

cause her to be carried away of the flood." There is, perhaps, a reference here to Isa. lix, 19: "When the enemy shall come in like a flood, the Spirit of the Lord shall lift up a standard against him." Looking back at that chapter, we shall find that the flood spoken of means an unusual increase of social disorders and crimes. That is most probably the meaning here. Satan is the foe alike of God and man. His enmity is directed as much against all order and morality as against goodness and righteousness. He is that "lawless one" of whom Paul speaks in 2 Thess. ii, 3 (Revised Version). If he were allowed to carry out his will he would subvert all government, spiritual or secular. But, says the apostle and seer, "The earth helped the woman." For its own protection and existence the State must execute laws, must preserve order, and must secure itself against anarchy and unbridled libertinism; and, in so far as it guards social morality, it fosters spiritual prosperity. In restraining crime and violence it must needs allow the kingdom of Christ opportunity to grow.

Foiled thus again, Satan does not abandon the conflict, but resorts to other and more wily means to make war with the "remnant" of the woman's seed "which keep the commandments of God, and have the testimony of Jesus Christ;" and the history of these efforts must next engage our attention.

2. *The First Wild Beast, or the Spirit of Worldliness.*—In the chapter of the Revelation which precedes the appearance of the beasts (Rev. xii, 12) the warning had been given, "Woe to the inhabiters of the earth and of the sea! for the devil is come down unto you, having great wrath." We are now to witness the fulfillment of this warning. The apostle saw two wild beasts rise, one from the sea, the other from the land, both of them formidable foes and intense in their hostility to the kingdom of Christ. There can hardly be a question but that these are intended to represent the means by which Satan, thwarted in his direct assaults, endeavors to carry on his warfare. And just as Christ, in carrying forward his mediatorial kingdom, makes use of the two instrumentalities, providence and the written word, so also, in imitation of him, his fierce antagonist has his two emissaries and agents. We shall find as we study this

The Foes of the Kingdom

part of the Revelation that one of the most deceptive and dangerous arts which Satan employs is his manner of counterfeiting the form and aping the methods of Christ, in hope that he may thereby delude the unsuspecting or heedless. We ought, therefore, very carefully to note every feature, that we may be able to detect these dangerous incarnations of the spirit of evil, and thus escape his snares.

The first wild beast of John's vision rose from the sea—an expression which, when used symbolically, designates the secular or temporal world, in antithesis to the Church. His distinctive characteristics are intense pride, the possession of vast power, strong vitality enabling him to recover speedily from severe injuries, insatiable craving after homage and ability to secure it, outrageous blasphemy, and undisguised as well as unceasing hostility to Christ and his saints. It is a mooted question whether by this beast John meant to describe and foretell the coming of some individual person or some organization of men, secular or religious, State or Church; or whether the characteristics he portrays are intended to represent some principle of evil, always at work, mightier and more enduring than any organization of men, which manifests itself in various forms and at all times, but transcends all its manifestations, and against which, because it is one of Satan's most successful means of antagonism, every Christian must keep perpetual watch.

The latter of these hypotheses seems to be more in keeping with the cast of John's strongly idealistic and abstract mind, and also with the purpose of the Apocalypse as intended for the edifying of believers. And furthermore, as the kingdom of God is not something that cometh " with observation," so that men can say of it, " Lo here! or, lo there!" but is something "within" us, so its opponent is not to be sought in any particular organization or special event or single individual, but rather in some abstract principle, all the more dangerous because it exists separate and distinct from these.

In his description of this wild beast John draws his data from the prophecy of Daniel; and a study of that book will aid in the elucidation of this. It is, indeed, true that in the mind of Daniel the antagonists and allies of God alike assumed the form of king-

The Foes of the Kingdom

doms, or world powers. But this resulted from the fact that his cast of mind was essentially concrete, and also because as a statesman and man of affairs, charged with the administration of finances and politics, accustomed to the handling of men in collective bodies and to deal with matters affecting their external relations, his conceptions of religion regarded rather its outward manifestations than its inward power. We are not, however, compelled to believe that John, while using the prophecies of Daniel as his basis, was limited to the conceptions of the older prophet. He had a better key to the hieroglyphics of the kingdom and could read their meaning more clearly. Behind the forces which play their part upon the world's stage he could recognize the spiritual principles of which they were incarnations.

The world power which loomed largest to the mind of Daniel, and whose hostility to the kingdom of Christ was most dreaded by him, was one that sprang up after the death and among the successors of Alexander the Great. That extraordinary captain and gifted statesman, the first ruler who grasped the conception of the essential unity of mankind and who strove to realize it by the fusion of races into one nation, left no one at his death capable of comprehending or executing his plans; and the empire that was formed by his ten generals was a heterogeneous one, possessing elements both of weakness and strength that were incapable of being welded into unity. Among the descendants and successors of these generals was Antiochus Epiphanes, whose hatred of Judaism amounted to real monomania, and whose insane purpose to exterminate utterly the customs, usages, religion, and even the existence of Judaism carried him to such extremes as to arouse a spirit of revolt which, under the guidance of the Maccabees, defeated his intent. In him the prophet Daniel foresaw the incarnation of all that is hostile to Christ and his kingdom.

In the days of John the political sovereignty of the world was wielded by a still more formidable power, one that combined in itself the strength of all the four kingdoms of Daniel, uniting the lion, the bear, and the leopard with the added and imparted authority and power of the dragon. That power was the Roman Empire, between which and Christianity had already begun

The Foes of the Kingdom

the antagonism which was to leave its decisive and disastrous effects upon both.

The policy of Rome toward conquered peoples and religions had not been one, customarily, of harsh severity; indeed, it had been marked in general by unusual liberality. Having so many gods in her own Pantheon, it has been said, the addition or subtraction of a few more or less was hardly worth consideration. But upon one thing Rome invariably and absolutely insisted—the preservation of public order. Her administration was one of strict, even stern, paternalism. The individual existed for the State, and had no rights but such as the State allowed. The central power did all the thinking; the subject had only to submit, whatever his personal wishes. Upon the emperor, as the embodiment of the State, devolved the onerous responsibility of securing and, if need were, of enforcing peaceful and lawful relations between men and men. Whenever therefore, the profession of any religion or the organization of any guild or association interfered with the prosperity of any branch of trade or commerce or manufacture, the emperor felt called upon to interpose, in order to redress the injury caused or wrong suffered thereby. The more conscientious and upright the emperor, the more he felt the responsibility of administering the laws; and thus just and righteous rulers, like Trajan and Antoninus and Marcus Aurelius, were more likely to enforce these rules of order, even to the point of persecution, than such men as Nero and Caligula and Domitian, upon whom moral considerations sat loosely.

The early persecutions of Christians sprang out of this fact. There were things Christian men would not do. They would not eat meat sacrificed to idols; they would not attend the spectacles of the theater; they would not worship or own images; and, as the trades and professions that lived by these things suffered with the increase of Christians, complaint was made to the emperor, and the power of the State invoked in behalf of public order. The riot at Ephesus (Acts xix, 23-41) is a case in illustration.

Very soon, however, the Roman authorities came to see that there was something back of Christian worship that differentiated it from other cults. There was a principle of individual liberty, a conviction of personal freedom, an appreciation of unseen and divine realities which, if unchecked, threatened the paternalism and the emperor —the worship of the Cæsars and the continuance of the empire; and so Christians began to be persecuted simply because they were Christians. Thus began the antagonism that did not cease until the empire became nominally Christian, and the Church, striving after the universality of the empire, became worldly and paternal in its turn. This antagonism John clearly discerned, and reveals it in the Apocalypse.

But we shall be astray if we conceive that the beast which the apostle saw symbolized only the Roman or any other empire. There is an evil principle which was in existence long before that empire was established, and has continued with unabating energy since its dissolution; of whose power earthly and worldly kingdoms are but manifestations; which Satan has employed in all ages as one of his most successful weapons; and whose deadly hostility to the Christian and the Church is implacable. It is the principle of worldliness, that spirit of the world against which the Bible so frequently and faithfully warns us.

It is not easy to define worldliness. If it could be described exactly, and its bounds accurately meted, its danger would be greatly diminished. If we could point to the doing or abstaining from doing of specified things, or the using or refraining from using of any particular faculties, and say, "This is worldliness and this only," how much easier it would be to avoid it! Worldliness is a principle, a spirit and temper of the soul. It can find a field for its exercise anywhere and everywhere, in things essentially good as well as in the essentially evil. Its intrinsic spirit lies in this—that it disengages men and things from their normal relation of dependence upon and subjection to God, and sets them up as rivals to him. It assumes to displace the Creator from his rightful sovereignty over thoughts and desires and affections and activities, and transfers allegiance to some created thing. It substitutes something temporal and earthly for God and gives to it the worship that belongs undividedly to him. It manifests itself, John tells us, in "the lust of the flesh, the lust of the eyes, and the vainglory of life." This is the spirit of which the Bible speaks so plainly and forcibly in passages like these: "If the world hate you, ye know that it hated me before it hated you;" "The carnal mind is enmity against God, for it is not subject to the law of God, neither indeed can be;" "Know ye not that the friendship of the world is enmity with God? whosoever, therefore, will be a friend of the world, is the enemy of God;" "If any man love the world, the love of the Father is not in him." And every characteristic of the wild beast which John saw exhibits this spirit of worldliness. It, and it alone, exhausts the fullness of the description.

Of this beast which John saw, one of the heads was, as it were, "wounded [or slain] to death"—the very words which were used in the description of the Lamb (Rev. v, 6), as if there were in this an attempted, although feeble, imitation of Christ. Worldliness, too, has its Calvaries and Gethsemanes; but they fall far short in measure and in purpose of the great sacrifice of the cross. They are compulsory, not self-chosen sacrifices; they are not redemptive and substitutional in their design, but retributive inflictions of divine justice; they involve but a part of the being, and are not, as was

Christ's offering, the surrender of the whole self.

Many such wounds has worldliness received. The serpent's head has been bruised again and again by the seed of the woman. In the judgments which have come upon the world throughout the course of its history—in the deluge, the destruction of Sodom and Gomorrah, the exodus from Egypt, the overthrow of Nineveh and Babylon, the fall of Jerusalem—its spirit has been rebuked, condemned, punished. Indeed, in all the dissolutions and decay of nature—in the fading of the grass, in the falling of the flower and of the leaf—the warning is being constantly given, "The world passeth away, and the lust thereof." Most of all, in the cross of Christ has the world received its deadliest wound. But how soon is the wound healed, how quickly are the lessons of providence forgotten! and the tide of worldliness, stayed for a moment, resumes its volume and rapidity and carries its victims to their destruction.

It is this power of recuperation which contributes to the might of worldliness and makes it the more dangerous. Success adds to its fascinations and multiplies its votaries.

The Foes of the Kingdom

"All the world wondered after the beast" whose deadly wound was healed. In comparison with its triumphs the cross of Christ becomes a stumbling-block to some and foolishness to others, because of the paucity of its victories. And in worshiping the beast its followers are scarcely aware, or are oblivious to the fact, that they are worshiping the dragon himself; for Paul says, "The things which the Gentiles sacrifice, they sacrifice to devils, and not to God."

Another striking and conspicuous characteristic of the first beast was his virulent blasphemy. Upon his heads were "the names of blasphemy." The voices of his mouth were blasphemy. His fierce, ambitious purpose to displace God and usurp his throne—and this is what the Bible defines blasphemy to be—moved him to demand such homage as can be given rightly to God alone, and to set up his own tabernacle and name as competitors with God's. Is not this descriptive of the spirit of worldliness? How exacting it is of the worship of its devotees! In place of the Creator, who is blessed for ever, it substitutes the creature. It enthrones nature in some one or other of its phases as the rival of the divine

Being. It will not admit the visible universe, with its laws, to be merely the vehicle through which God reveals himself and his thoughts, but demands for it equality of homage with its Maker. It does not claim for itself power to work miracles, and will not believe that any are possible. It does not base its authority upon any supernatural revelation, and denies that any is needful. Like Absalom, in the gates it whispers in every man's ears, "O that I were made judge in the land!" and thus draws unwary souls into treason against their King. It arrogates to itself the right to the whole of man's being—to all beauty and life, to all literature and art, to all recreation and enjoyment, to the exclusive and undivided use and administration of all earthly powers and faculties.

And how ruthless and cruel this spirit of worldliness can be! Does any human soul, driven by dissatisfaction and heartache, seek to lift the veil and penetrate to the secret shrine of the universe, or to pierce the "rose mesh" of mystery that surrounds us and ascend to the divine Spirit above and beyond it, how quickly is the fascinating smile of the world turned to bitter scorn, and its

The Foes of the Kingdom

smooth flattery to remorseless persecution! With what haughtiness and assumption does it contend that, in everything relating to music and poetry, to the æsthetic arts, to finance and politics and social matters, the question of morals has no place and God and religion have no right to enter!

To this beast, we are further informed, power, or authority, was given " to continue forty and two months." This number, it has been previously said, is the symbol of an epoch which is limited and fractional, but which has a definite purpose pervading it.

Throughout the whole period of Judaism this beast raged with all his ferocity against the Church of the Old Testament. And, although the wild beast next to be delineated was a more formidable adversary to religion than even he, yet the temptation to fall into the ways, and follow the practices, and to drop down to the religious level of the ungodly world of heathenism around constituted a peril to the Hebrew faith against which the prophets had need frequently to lift their voices. And how constant even now is the peril to the Christian Church and the Christian believer of falling into the worship of the same beast of worldliness, is so patent a truth that every man's observation and experience are sufficient to prove it. The victims of worldliness are, indeed, many, and to resist sorely tries "the patience and the faith of the saints." But its doom is sure and irretrievable, whether that doom shall come by the sword of God or by captivity. Its own methods of hostility shall be turned against itself.

3. *The Second Wild Beast, or the Spirit of False Prophetism.*—In attempting to solve the mystery of the second wild beast which John saw we are confronted with a task much more serious than has as yet been presented to us. Not only is this antagonist of Christ a more formidable one than any hitherto encountered, but there seems an almost purposed obscurity and indistinctness about the description, as if to the seer himself the beast appeared in so vague and nebulous a form, or else was of such composite and heterogeneous character, as to be incapable of more exact delineation. The only way to reach the truth is to seek out such features of the description as may be regarded plain, and from them to advance to the more perplexing ones.

It will be noticed, then, that the second beast rises not as the preceding from the sea, but from the earth; that is, from the Church, not in its ideal state, but in its actual condition, as the field of human activity and influence.

Again, it is noticeable that, while in the description of the first beast the expression "it was given him" occurs again and again (much more conspicuously in the original than in the translation), in the case of the second one this expression is, in the main, although not in every instance, superseded by words suggesting active agency—"he doeth," "he maketh," "he causeth"—these being all various renderings of the same Greek word. This would seem to imply that, while the first beast is merely an emissary or instrument executing the will of another, the second differs from him in that he has, or assumes to have, some power of originating action, some causative agency, and that he regards himself as having independent authority. While, therefore, the results effected by both are the same ("He had power to give breath to the image of the beast"), those results are brought about in different ways.

Another very important feature of the description is that, while the distinguishing characteristic of the first beast is blasphemy—an open and undisguised assumption of the prerogatives of God, with intense and avowed hostility to him—the properties of the second are duplicity, deception, and self-deceit—perversion of the truth rather than antagonism to it; and hypocrisy, if more insidious, is far deadlier than open opposition. He has the appearance of a lamb, while speaking as a dragon. He is said to work miracles, or at least is said to profess so to do, which the first beast did not. And he counterfeits the work of God, in that by a peculiar mark he stamps upon his followers his claim to them, as the divine Being affixes to his a seal in attestation of his ownership.

One further remark may be made. Three times in the subsequent part of the Revelation (Rev. xvi, 13; xix, 20; xx, 10) these two adversaries of Christ are brought into juxtaposition, and in these instances it is the first beast alone who is designated by that name. The second beast has the synonym of "the false prophet." The term seems to mark his superior power or craft;

The Foes of the Kingdom

to the malice of a beast is added the higher intelligence of a man. The combination attests the formidable character of this wily antagonist.

In this last-named feature lies a suggestion which may serve as a clew to the interpretation of the symbol and unveil its mystery. A false prophet can stand only in contrast with a true one. It will be needful, therefore, to discuss, somewhat in detail, the characteristic functions of the prophetical office as set forth in the Scriptures.

"The usage of the word [prophet]," says Cremer,* "is clear. It signifies one to whom and through whom God speaks. What really constitutes the prophet is immediate intercourse with God, a divine communication of what the prophet must declare. Two things, therefore, go to make the prophet—an insight granted by God into the divine secrets or mysteries, and a communication to others of those secrets. New Testament prophets were for the Christian Church what Old Testament prophets were for Israel, inasmuch as they maintained intact the immediate connection between the

Lexicon of New Testament Greek, third English edition, pp. 568, 569.

Church and, not the Holy Spirit in her, but the God of her salvation above her. The prophets, both in the old and the new dispensations, were messengers or media of communication between the upper and the lower world."

"The primary idea of a prophet," says Ewald,* "is of one who has seen or heard something which does not concern himself, or not himself alone, which will not let him rest. It wholly absorbs him, . . . so that he no longer hears or is conscious of himself, but of the loud and clear voice of another who is higher than himself. He acts and speaks, not of his own accord; a higher one impels him, to resist whom is sin. It is his God, who is also the God of those to whom he must speak."

"That which," says Oehler,† "made the prophet a prophet was not his natural gifts nor his own intention; and that which he proclaimed as the prophetic word was not the mere result of instruction received nor the product of his own reflection. The

---

Prophets of the Old Testament, vol. i, p. 7. London, Williams and Norgate.

†*Theology of the Old Testament*, §§ 205, 206. New York, Funk and Wagnalls.

prophet, as such, knows himself to be the organ of divine revelation, in virtue both of a divine vocation capable of being known by him as such, . . . and also of his endowment with the enlightening, sanctifying, and strengthening Spirit of God."

With these statements the concurrent testimony of the New Testament is in harmony: "God . . . at sundry times and in divers manners spake in time past unto the fathers by the prophets" (Heb. i, 1); "The prophecy came not in old time by the will of man: but holy men of God spake as they were moved by the Holy Ghost" (2 Pet. i, 21).

It was, therefore, essential to the credibility and authority of the prophet that he should have received some direct revelation from God. The message intrusted to him to deliver must be from a source above and outside himself. It was not sufficient that God spake in him; he must be able to say that God spake to him. When to the student prepared by the guidance of a teacher to receive them nature reveals its facts and laws, these come to him as something external to him. They are not suggestions or inspirations of his own mind, but owe their origin to a source exterior to it. So likewise with the prophet. How the revelation came to him, and how his hearers became convinced that God had spoken to him, are questions that do not touch the truth of his message. The important thing is that the prophet was the agent and representative of God in delivering a message which had previously been committed to him. Herein lay the distinction between the priesthood and the prophetical office. A priest was a man on whom was laid the responsibility of appearing before God on behalf of men; a prophet was one who stood in the presence of men on behalf of God. A priest represented man in the court of God; a prophet represented God in the court of human life. A priest was man's advocate; a prophet was God's advocate. The function of the priest was to intercede for his fellows; identity of condition and tender sympathy with them were therefore prime requisites. The function of a prophet was to deliver God's word to man; strict fidelity to his message and to the truth were his essential qualifications. As the priesthood, then, was a type of Christ, finding its perfect realization in him who laid down

The Foes of the Kingdom

his life a ransom for us, the prophetical office was a type of the Holy Ghost, whose work it is to convey to man the message of God, whether it be of conviction, of justification, of sanctification, of inspiration, or of assurance.

If, therefore, by a "false Christ" is meant one who usurps the place of Christ and substitutes himself for him, demanding from men the allegiance due only to the Son of God, then by a "false prophet" must be meant one who unconsciously or purposely substitutes himself for the Holy Spirit, setting forth his own conceptions or visions as the voice of God.

"The characteristic," says Oehler,* "of the false prophets is declared to be that they speak that which they themselves have devised. These latter are designated (Ezek. xiii, 2) as prophets 'out of their own hearts,' who 'follow their own spirit, and have seen nothing;' 'they speak,' according to Jer. xxiii, 16, "a vision of their own heart, and not out of the mouth of the Lord.'"

No stage of history has been free from such presumptuous prophets. Their exist-

* *Theology of the Old Testament*, p. 464.

ence and the disastrous work they wrought are set forth again and again in the Old Testament Scriptures. But that their appearance in larger numbers and under more formidable guises may be expected in the New Testament dispensation follows from a consideration of the influence of Christianity upon human nature.

Unquestionably, one marked result of that copious effusion of the Holy Spirit, which beginning at Pentecost has continued until now, was a quickening of the human soul to a realization of its individuality. Fifteen centuries of sad experience and a convulsion which disrupted Western Christendom were needed to bring any large portion of the Church to an appreciation of the privileges which inhere in this individualism. Since the great Reformation of the sixteenth century, men have come by freer study of the Bible to discern more clearly the possibilities which it teaches of personal consciousness of sonship, and of the individual possession by the Holy Spirit of every soul availing itself of the privilege; although there have never been wanting those who have discerned the possibility of individual communion with the spiritual world.

The Foes of the Kingdom

In individualism lurks a danger against which no revelation can absolutely secure us. I may transgress its prescribed limitations and become excessive. It may strive after independence from its Creator and put forth its hands to forbidden fruit. It may assume prerogatives which the divine Being reserves to himself. It may substitute its own imaginings and volitions for voices of God, and displace that real spirituality which only the Holy Ghost can create with an auto-spiritualism which is deceptive, illusory, and specious, the precursor of spiritual and intellectual anarchy.

Our Lord gave warning of this peril when, predicting the trials which should come, he said, "There shall arise false Christs, and false prophets, and shall show great signs and wonders; insomuch that, if it were possible, they shall deceive the very elect." Paul foresaw it, saying to the Ephesian elders, "Of your own selves shall men arise, speaking perverse things, to drawaway disciples after them." It was this which led John to write, "Believe not every spirit, but try the spirits whether they are of God: because many false prophets are gone out into the world."

Revelation of Saint John

The writer of the Revelation had no need to go beyond his own memory to find symptoms of this spirit. Already it had begun to manifest itself in the apostolic Church. Simon Magus was a conspicuous but not solitary example. In the epistles to the seven churches there are cautions against "the Nicolaitans" and "the woman Jezebel, which calleth herself a prophetess," very distinct from those which denounce the pleasures or the persecutions of the world. In the ante-Nicene age gnosticism, with its pretensions to a theosophy more profound, a knowledge more extensive and exact, a code of ethics more consistent, and a self-denial more rigid than those of the faithful, was a more dangerous adversary than the Roman empire; and we who appreciate the skillfulness of its specious arguments realize that nothing but the providence of God carried the artless and unsuspicious Church safely through the peril.* And throughout the ages since there has been a continuous reappearance of this spirit, sometimes within, sometimes

---

* Bigg, *Christian Platonists of Alexandria*, Bampton Lectures, 1886, lecture i, p. 35 ; Harnack, *History of Dogma*, book i, chapt. iv.

The Foes of the Kingdom

outside the Church; not always avowedly antagonistic to Christianity, but assuming to be a more perfect form of it; not impugning the authority of the Scriptures, but claiming to possess deeper views of their esoteric meaning; not openly subverting the foundations of morals, but superseding them by a show of a more austere and uncompromising sanctimoniousness. It so puts on the appearance of a lamb that its dragon nature is hard to detect. It has cropped out in Manichæism, in Paulicianism, in Albigensianism, among hermits and pillar saints, among pietists, mystics, occultists, and other professors of a strained and exalted perfection and illumination to which only the elect initiate can aspire, and from which the common masses of believers are excluded.

It is hard to describe this spirit by a single name. It wears so many forms that no one word can comprehend all of them. Even the apostolic pen failed to depict this adversary clearly or sketch its outline with distinctness. Deceit seems to be the pervading and controlling element of its being, and to affect both substance and form. But it has as its usual accompaniment one mark which it stamps upon its devotees—a scrupulous and rigid asceticism which deludes itself with the hope of emancipation from the necessary conditions of earthly life, which denounces as sinful things proper in themselves, simply because they are natural or secular, and which aims at the profitless and impracticable task of anticipating in this life the celestial state of disembodied spirits. No creature can ever with impunity contravene the laws imposed upon his nature. The abnormal and excessive development of one side of man's constitution is sure to involve a corresponding atrophy of some other side, and thus the sins excluded by one system of defenses find entrance through some other avenue left unguarded. And the constant result of asceticism has been in the end to revive with new power the worldliness it aimed to destroy; so that in this sense the second beast gives "life" and breath "unto the image" of the first. For the termination of all hyperspiritualism has been either in an arrogant self-exaltation, the very opposite of Christian humility and love, or in an antinomianism which, under the affectation of liberty, gives loose rein to sensualism.

The Foes of the Kingdom

To the question, which thus becomes of vital importance, How shall we "try the spirits" to know "whether they are of God"? John has elsewhere furnished a sufficient answer: "Every spirit that confesseth that Jesus Christ is come in the flesh is of God: and every spirit that confesseth not that Jesus Christ is come in the flesh is not of God: and this is that spirit of antichrist, whereof ye have heard that it should come; and even now already is it in the world" (1 John iv, 2, 3).

The central principle of all asceticism, in whatever form, and whether perceived and acknowledged or not, is that matter is essentially evil and spirit essentially good. It is in the contact of soul with body and of spirit with matter that sin lies. Holiness, therefore, means only the diminution or destruction of this contact. All bodily desires, activities, and enjoyments, if they cannot be annihilated, must be reduced to the minimum, that thereby the ascendency of the spirit may be gained and maintained. Thus human nature is mutilated to half its capacities. Religion becomes only a "concision," not a process of transformation. The problem of redemption is no longer the moral one of the salvation of the soul from the guilt and pollution of sin, but the metaphysical one of the liberation of the spirit from matter.* By such as hold this view of things the assumption by the Son of God of the likeness of sinful flesh, his birth, his fellowship with earthly conditions and experiences, can never be fully accepted; his crucifixion is attenuated into a figure of speech or becomes a mere parable, and cannot be the necessary means of our salvation.

Against such a theory the Revelation is one long protest. Its keynote is salvation through "the Lamb that was slain." Nor does anything prove so conclusively that John was the author of the Apocalypse as the fact that in it, in the fourth gospel, and in the epistles which bear his name, the central and fundamental truth was the same: "The Word was made flesh, and dwelt among us;" and, "This is he that came by water and blood, even Jesus Christ; not by water only, but by water and blood. And it is the Spirit that beareth witness, because the Spirit is truth."

*Möller, *History of the Christian Church*, vol. i, pp. 152, 153. New York, Swan Sonnenschein & Co., 1892.

The acquisition of knowledge depends as much upon a right method as upon an earnest purpose. Alphabets must be mastered before sentences can be read. No one can understand the higher mathematics who has not been grounded in the fundamental axioms. And one of the axioms of the spiritual life is that the Holy Spirit cannot be given until Jesus is glorified (John vii, 39). Whoever does not accept, with all implied therein, the exemplary earthly life and the atoning and sacrificial death of the Son of God may well pause to reflect whether the spirit which leads and moves him is indeed the Spirit of God, or whether it is not the spirit of evil and untruth. We may not set limits to the spiritual flights of which the soul is capable, but it must have a solid basis from which to start; otherwise it wastes its strength in aimless wanderings amid mazy fogs and vagaries.

The path of truth lies between extremes, and from either side of the ridge along which it winds steep declines lead to dangerous abysses. If a man, on the one hand, accepts to the full the reality of the incarnation of the Son of God, and then does not advance to that other revealed truth, that the

Holy Ghost is of equal power and divinity and that his mission is as wide in its range and as complete in its effects, religion will be to him a thing of externals, of outward and mechanical forms and rites. On the other hand, the ascetic who would aspire to the full heights of the revelation of the Holy Spirit without accepting what must precede success—the real humanity of our Lord, his cross, his grave, his resurrection—will surely miss the path and be lost in abstractions, fanaticisms, delusion, and deceit.

One last feature descriptive of the second beast remains to be considered—the number of his name. "Let him that hath understanding count the number of the beast: for it is the number of a man; and his number is six hundred threescore and six." If John meant to cover a mystery he has certainly succeeded, for no explanation has as yet been offered convincing enough to command the acceptance of the Church. Unquestionably this is the most difficult to solve of all the problems of the book, and the apostle is thought to intimate this in saying, "Here is wisdom;" although possibly his meaning is that the special need for wisdom lies in defense against the wiles of

The Foes of the Kingdom

this adversary, rather than in solving the mystery of his name.

The interpretation which has met with the largest assent is based on the usage of employing the letters of the Greek and Hebrew alphabets as numerals. Men have attempted to discover some name the letters of which when added will give the numerical value six hundred and sixty-six. The name which has secured the largest number of advocates is Lateinos (Latin), which, written in Greek characters and numbered, gives six hundred and sixty-six. By Roman Catholic interpreters who accept this solution the empire of Rome is supposed to be meant; by Protestants, the Church of Rome. Dr. Adam Clarke thought this solution to "amount nearly to demonstration."

In recent times many German and other scholars, mainly for reasons based on a special theory of the date of the Revelation, prefer the words Nero Cæsar, which, written in Hebrew letters, number six hundred and sixty-six. Irenæus (died about 202), who attempted the problem, out of many names preferred Teitan, possibly to suggest an analogy between the attempts of

Roman emperors to crush the Church and the unsuccessful war of the Titans against the gods, without venturing to put forth his opinions in more definite form. Very many other names of men, ancient and modern, have been proposed, with greater or less plausibility; for curiosity to decipher numerical symbols, when it possesses a man, holds him with almost the fascination of gambling. But it is apparent that the combination of names possible with only a few letters is so much beyond computation that almost apostolical inspiration is requisite to decide upon the right one.

To the word "Lateinos," strong as are its claims, the objection lies that the Roman or Latin empire can scarcely be meant, since the beast John describes is evidently a spiritual power, not a secular one. Nor can the Roman Church be meant, for it was not known as Latin in the days of the apostle, nor for centuries afterward; and, as one design of the Apocalypse was to comfort and instruct the generation in which John lived, it would have been inconsistent with that design to select a name which could have no meaning intelligible to it or to many generations succeeding. There is wisdom in

The Foes of the Kingdom

the words of Bleek:* "The discovery that a definite name contains this number as the value of its letters in Greek would not warrant us to assume the correctness of the interpretation if other hints in the book respecting the beast did not agree."

Another explanation offered is that the number six hundred and sixty-six is but a threefold repetition of the number six, John thus intending to mark in the most emphatic manner that, however mighty the power or long the duration of the beast shall be, it will inevitably fall short of the completeness and permanence of Christ's kingdom, as six is less than seven.

Still another explanation proposed is that the number was originally written with the Greek letters χξς; χ being equal to six hundred, ξ to sixty, and ς to six. As χ (*ch*) is the initial letter of Christ, ξ is supposed to be an emblem of Satan, being afterward so used by the Gnostics, and ς is the initial of σταυρός, *cross*. The symbol, it is said, refers to some Satanic power intervening between Christ and the cross, some system which honors him as teacher but denies

* *Lectures on the Apocalypse*, p. 87. London, Williams & Norgate, 1875.

him as Saviour, which accepts Jesus, but not "him crucified." The description accords well enough with that of the second beast; but whether it can be extracted from the number six hundred and sixty-six is another question. The monogram, while harmonizing with the symbolism of the Apocalypse, and also delineating the nature of the beast, does not explain the emphasis which seems to be laid upon his "name."

There is, however, one detail in this part of the description of the beast often overlooked, but which may carry us far on our way to decipher the secret of the number. The number of the name is not monopolized by the beast; it does not exhaust itself in any single individual. We are told that " no man might buy or sell, save he that had the mark, or the name of the beast, or the number of his name." The beast has followers who imbibe his spirit and partake of his characteristics, and to whom his name and number are equally appropriate. It is more in keeping with this statement, as well as with other details, to interpret the beast as a principle rather than a person, as being some spirit of evil which, assuming

The Foes of the Kingdom

prominence in some man or organization, is yet shared by many men and organizations. The ascetic, false prophetism which fulfills the other details of the description coincides also with this.

If, following out the rule of interpretation which has guided us hitherto, and assuming that John drew his prediction of the future from facts and tendencies existing in his day, we read the epistles contained in chapters ii and iii, we shall find that among the perils which threatened the apostolic Church none was more imminent than that which is called "the doctrine of the Nicolaitans," which was but a reproduction of the heresy of Balaam, the gifted and formidable rival and antagonist of Moses; the name Nicolaus, indeed, meaning in Greek the same that Balaam does in Hebrew. So deep a mark did Balaam make that throughout the Old Testament, as well as the New, he stands as the representative, as he was the first example, of that spirit of false prophetism which, beginning as asceticism, degenerates into antinomianism and prostitutes genius to the service of the flesh. Now, it is certainly true, as Züllig shows,*

* *Bleek, Lectures on the Apocalypse*, p. 285.

that the words " Balaam, the son of Beor, soothsayer," if written in Hebrew letters do make up the sum six hundred and sixty-six. It seems, therefore, probable that some embodiment of his insidious spirit, some reproduction of his deadly doctrine, with its resultant lawless practices, is the solution of this mysterious symbol, the second beast, against which John earnestly warns the Church in all ages to guard itself as the most dangerous foe to the kingdom of Christ. And possibly the archæological researches which are now bringing to light much of the hidden history of earlier ages may yet discover to us the sect which served as the basis of his warning.

The interpretation which has here been put upon the symbols of the two wild beasts—namely, that they represent, the one the spirit of worldliness, the other that autospiritualism or self-centered piety which, for lack of a more comprehensive phrase, may be designated as false prophetism or false asceticism—derives some confirmation from the fact that their resulting effects have been such as the author of the Revelation predicted. Worldliness seems the baser of the two, but its dominion is

The Foes of the Kingdom

briefer and less stable. As the mind can never be content with agnosticism,. but must by necessity search for some explanation of the mystery of being until satisfaction is gained, so the heart can never fully rest in hopes and themes and joys which are only earthly. The religious instincts inherent in and inalienable from our nature will assert themselves and cry for God. On the other hand, asceticism, while it seems to present a loftier ideal and holds men thereby with a more permanent grasp, is all the more baleful by reason of its deceptiveness. It veils pride, ambition, malice, selfishness, under the guise of superior sanctity, which, while imposing on others by its well-masked duplicity, lulls its victims into almost hopeless slumber by its hypocrisy. Those whom it allures by its professions of superior piety it mocks with disappointing dreams. It is the dark shadow that always waits on holiness and liberty ; it is the special temptation that besets souls seeking after purity and knowledge; while worldliness is that to which those are most prone who mingle much with the world and deal with earthly realities. If, on the one hand, it is easy for men to fall into the danger of using their heaven-given faculties for the ignoble purpose of gratifying their lower desires or of turning stones to bread simply that they may live, it is equally easy, on the other, to wander into the opposite error of presuming rashly upon God's providence and mercy, although humility has degenerated into boasting and love has been perverted to censoriousness. From neither tendency can the regeneration of the world come; both are alike enemies of God and of man.

4. *Anticipations of Victory.*—It is one of the characteristic peculiarities of St. John's literary style to introduce a subject which for the moment he merely suggests to our notice, returning to it subsequently in order that he may amplify and complete it. He goes over his work again and again, each time adding some new touch, with the purpose of bringing out in greater prominence some detail of his subject. While each section, therefore, contains in measure an epitome of the whole, in each one some single point is more specifically and elaborately discussed. There is, it is true, advance of thought; but the eagle of the apostolic band moves in circles, bringing into notice of his keen eye every part of the field over

which he soars, while each swoop of his wing carries him a little beyond his former orbit, so that his progress is in spirals. The principle which controlled him seems to have been that of presenting to us in sharp and striking antithesis the contrasts between conflicting ideas, while he holds them under our observation.

It is also characteristic of a disposition like St. John's, and of a life so contemplative and secluded as his was, to view things in the light of their essential principles; not as they become, modified by contact and in relation with each other, but as they radically and germinally are. By consequence such minds, instead of being occupied with the intermediate changes, pass at once to ultimate results and see the end in the beginning.

An instance of this appears in the fourteenth chapter, which is really but an epilogue to the preceding chapters. In the twelfth and thirteenth chapters we have had presented to our vision the formidable enemies with which the Christian believer must struggle. They have been described most graphically and with a fullness of detail not subsequently exceeded. The *dramatis personæ* are all put upon the stage, and no new actors in the tragedy of existence need be expected. But these enemies are sufficiently numerous and terrible to excite apprehension and awaken earnest inquiries as to our means of resistance and possibilities of success. The seer, therefore, pauses for a moment to review the resources put within our reach and to assure us of their adequacy. "Greater is he that is in you," he says, "than he that is in the world." And he fully indorses the emphatic declaration of Paul, "The weapons of our warfare are not carnal, but mighty through God to the pulling down of strongholds."

In prophesying victory over the dragon and the beasts to the saints of Christ, John separates them into two classes, as he had done in chapter vii. This is not in any spirit of Jewish narrowness or exclusiveness. He had long gotten beyond that and learned to call no man common whom God had cleansed. Even Paul, the apostle of the uncircumcision, recognized a distinction between the Jew, who was first, and the Gentile; so there can be alleged against John no bigotry in recognizing the distinction,

The Foes of the Kingdom

inasmuch as he foreshadows equal victory to both classes. There can hardly be a question that by the "hundred forty and four thousand" John meant Israelites after the flesh; for they "stood on the mount Sion;" they sang a song which none others but themselves could learn, namely, the song of Moses and of the Lamb (xv, 3); they were "the first fruits unto God and to the Lamb" (xiv, 4); they were without "guile," with reference no doubt to John i, 47. They were "virgins," having the true asceticism—freedom from ungodliness and worldly lusts. There was reason for rejoicing to a Jew like John in the fact that, in spite of the opposition of the rulers and Herods among the chosen people to whom had been committed the oracles of God, and on the very spots of the crucifixion and resurrection, so many of his former coreligionists had become disciples of Christ and followed the Lamb whithersoever he led them.

But the word of God is not bound, nor is it the exclusive property of any race; and the seer immediately adds the vision of the multitudes of "every nation, and kindred, and tongue, and people," to whom "the everlasting Gospel" was preached and among whom it found adherents. The fullness of the times had come, and Gentiles might "fear God, and give glory to him," the one Creator of "heaven, and earth, and the sea, and the fountains of waters."

One new feature is now introduced. Babylon, which occupies so much of the subsequent part of the Apocalypse, is here for the first time mentioned. Babylon, it will be attempted to show, is not another adversary, but an apostate Church which has succumbed to adversaries and thereby become a counterfeit and rival to Christianity. It is here brought upon the stage by anticipation, and its doom foretold, to give completer assurance of the coming victory over all forms and results of sin and evil.

The age in which John lived was an age of martyrdom. How severely this fact tried "the patience" and faith of the early Christians we know from hints in other apostolical writings. Paul found it necessary to show to his brethren in Rome that if they suffered with Christ it was that they might be also glorified together with him. Peter, too, comforts those whose faith was being so sorely tried with the assurance

The Foes of the Kingdom

that the trial of their faith was "more precious than of gold that perisheth," and would be "found unto praise and honor and glory at the appearing of Jesus Christ." And so John gives to the Church of his day the glad tidings that, although God buries his workmen, he carries on his work; that they, if they died "in the Lord," should "rest from their labors;" and that "their works" should survive and go on winning victories after their departure.

If it should be asked how or with what weapons they were to overcome, John gives the answer which is found so often in the Book of Revelation that it is one of the keys to unlock its mysteries—they overcome "by the blood of the Lamb, and by the word of their testimony" (Rev. xii, 11); by which latter expression is meant, doubtless, the Scriptures, as explained in the chapter upon the two witnesses. That the two visions which now follow, the harvest of the world and the vintage scene, refer to these two weapons of success furnishes an explanation of them so simple and easy that it is strange they should have occasioned so much difficulty to commentators.

The prophet Joel, from whose writings

these visions are drawn (Joel iii, 13), probably among the earliest and certainly among the greatest of the Hebrew seers, appears to have been gifted with a foresight of the future remarkable even for one of that extraordinary body of men. The final and complete triumph of God's cause over all opposing foes in and through Zion, and the deliverance of the Church from all bondage, oppression, and danger, preceded by a plentiful outpouring of the Holy Spirit upon all classes, ages, and conditions, stood out before him as a certain and assured fact. The details of the methods by which this result was to be achieved were not revealed to him, nor is it surprising that, being thus left to himself, he could conceive of no other instrumentalities than those which in his experience of human affairs had passed under his own observation. This is not the only instance in which the apostles of the New Testament, while confirming the prophets of the Old as to results, have discerned more clearly the power of spiritual forces, and for swords and carnal weapons and rods of iron have substituted the more peaceful instrumentalities of the sword of the Spirit, the breath

The Foes of the Kingdom

of the Messiah's lips, and the staff of the Good Shepherd.

The writer of the Revelation, expanding and evangelizing the vision of Joel, saw "a white cloud," and One "like unto the Son of man" sitting thereon, "having on his head a golden crown, and in his hand a sharp sickle." "Out of the temple" an angel came and cried to him, "Thrust in thy sickle, . . . for the harvest of the earth is ripe." Whereupon he cast his sickle upon the earth, and "the earth was reaped."

In these words surely a reference is to be seen to the words of our Lord himself uttered in the hearing of John and recorded in Matt. xxiv, 14, 30, 31: "And this Gospel of the kingdom shall be preached in all the world for a witness unto all nations; and then shall the end come. . . . And they shall see the Son of man coming in the clouds of heaven with power and great glory. And he shall send his angels with a great sound of a trumpet, and they shall gather together his elect from the four winds, from one end of heaven to the other."

This metaphor of the harvest as the result of the sowing of God's word is one of the most common to be found in the Scriptures. "The sower soweth the word" (Mark iv, 14), or "the word of the kingdom" (Matt. xiii, 19), or "the word which by the Gospel is preached unto you" (1 Peter i, 25). "So is the kingdom of God, as if a man should cast seed into the ground; and should sleep, and rise night and day, and the seed should spring and grow up, he knoweth not how. For the earth bringeth forth fruit of herself [that is, automatically and spontaneously]. . . . But when the fruit is brought forth, immediately he putteth in the sickle, because the harvest is come" (Mark iv, 26–29).

That "the word of God is quick and powerful" (Heb. iv, 12); that it has God's life in it (John vi, 63); that it is the great weapon of warfare, defensive and offensive, to the Church and the believer; that it is the incorruptible seed by which men are born into the kingdom (1 Peter i, 23); that it is the instrument whereby we are sanctified (John xvii, 17), is the concurrent declaration of the Scriptures themselves. That it is to be preached by apostles, prophets, pastors, and teachers is the commission binding on all: "Go ye into all the world, and preach the Gospel to every creature" (Mark xvi, 15).

The Foes of the Kingdom

This Bible is sufficient of itself, all other things are only ancillary; "in due season we shall reap, if we faint not" (Gal. vi, 9). All literature and art and culture and science are but as "the grass" that "withereth," or "the flower" that "fadeth;" "but the word of our God shall stand forever." And the martyrs of the apostolical age had the inspired assurance of John to console them, that if they faithfully bore witness to the word they might fall, but "their works" would follow on after them. And in so saying he is only reëchoing the words which he himself had heard from the Master, "One soweth, and another reapeth" (John iv, 37). And John shows how completely he had gotten away from Jewish narrowness and absorbed the Master's spirit, in his recognition of the fact that the Bible is for every nation and kindred and people.

The other instrumentality of victory put within the reach of the Church, namely, the all-sufficient "blood of the Lamb," is beautifully illustrated in the vintage vision, which has most needlessly perplexed commentators.

An angel—not now the Son of man—is seen coming "out of the temple which is in heaven" with a sharp sickle. Another angel came out from the altar, who is described as having "power over fire" (the same combination as is found in Isa. vi, 6), and at his cry the sickle was thrust into the earth, and the clusters of fully ripe grapes gathered and cast "into the great wine press of the wrath of God."

It is hardly possible to read these words without seeing in them a reference to Isa. lxiii, 1–6. By the great mass of believers the words are interpreted as an allusion to and a prophecy of the atoning work of Christ. It certainly seems that the writer of the Revelation so understood them, not only from the connection of this vintage scene with the blood of the Lamb, but also from Rev. xix, 11–16, where the same connection of the two themes, the "sharp sword" issuing from the mouth of Christ, that is, the word of God, and the "vesture dipped in blood," with the treading of the wine press, is found.

Our belief in the plenary inspiration of the writers of the Scriptures does not compel us to the conviction that they always comprehended the full import of their message, or that all the particulars embraced

The Foes of the Kingdom

therein stood out clearly and plainly in their minds. This is one of the instances in which prophets and wise men desired to see the things which we in the kingdom of Christ see, but did not see them. Every man in painting mental pictures must of necessity use colors with which his own mind is acquainted, and which he has acquired by experience and observation. And Isaiah and the other prophets, in the age and with the surroundings in the midst of which they lived, had no other means of conveying to the minds of men the true revelations which were given to them of the suffering and victorious Messiah than terms such as they saw exemplified in the world of history and in the men about them. Any other terms would have been incomprehensible, and so have failed of their purpose to help and inspirit. And the divinity of the Bible is seen conspicuously in this—that the framework in which its glorious pictures were set is capable of expansion to the times in which we live and the larger views we have, without fracture or distortion. The signs and symbols which by divine illumination were presented to them have come down to us; but we, with the clearer light of the Sun of righteousness, can read intelligently what were hieroglyphics to them, and, looking with unveiled face, can behold therein the glory of God. That John, in thus quoting from Isaiah, has Calvary and Gethsemane in his thoughts is shown by his specifying particularly that "the wine press was trodden without the city," bringing out the truth, of which Heb. xiii, 12, is the witness, that "Jesus also, that he might sanctify the people with his own blood, suffered without the gate."

It is true that in the prophecy of Isaiah there appears an element of vengeance and wrath that does not comport with our ideas of salvation and redemption, and even repels. The element is still there; but the New Testament teaches us that all that was lonely, painful, agonizing in human redemption was borne by the Christ for us. We are "bought with a price," but he paid it. He was "made a curse for us." He "bare our sins in his own body on the tree," and by his "stripes" we are "healed." However feeble may be the traces of vicariousness in nature, human life is full of it, is built about it. All love is manifested in vicarious suffering. Scarce any rise but

The Foes of the Kingdom

that some fall; scarce any become rich but that others become poor; there is hardly a smile or a laugh of joy for which some pain is not felt or some tear not shed somewhere. And, if God manifests his love by sending "his Son to be the propitiation for our sins," this is but an illustration of the truth, as apparent in the spiritual world as in that of nature, of the transmutation of forces; the sum not being increased or diminished, but the places and modes of manifestation changing.

The remainder of the vintage scene may be easily explained, difficult as it has seemed to most interpreters, by applying the key which is put into our hands, if we accept the solution offered above.

We must now for almost the first time take up the prophecy of Ezekiel, which from this place onward almost singly rules the Apocalypse, and the careful study of which will throw light upon what seems most obscure.

We are told that "blood came out of the wine press, even unto the horse bridles, by the space of a thousand and six hundred furlongs."

Turning to Ezekiel, we find that the last

chapters of that great prophecy are taken up with a beautiful description, ideal and figurative, doubtless, of the restored temple, holy city, and land of the new Israel of God. In the forty-seventh chapter of Ezekiel the dimensions of this ideal land are very carefully stated. The boundary line of it was, on the north side, Hamath, in latitude thirty-four degrees twenty minutes, and, on the south, a line drawn from Tamar, at the southern border of the Dead Sea, to Kadesh, a brook emptying into the Mediterranean. If, now, we measure on a map the distance between these lines, we shall find it to be two hundred miles, or sixteen hundred furlongs.

This whole space, comprehending all of the Holy Land, was thus entirely covered with the blood which flowed from the wine press trodden by the Son of God. Could there be a more complete statement of the all-sufficiency of that atoning blood? It is the same truth presented to us here which John has elsewhere in plainer prose revealed to our faith: "The blood of Jesus Christ his Son cleanseth us from all sin."

And as if still further to verify the statement he tells us that the blood reached to "the horse bridles." There is an allusion in this to Zech. xiv, 20, where we are told that in "the day of the Lord" there shall be "upon the bells [or, as the margin has it, 'upon the bridles'] of the horses, Holiness unto the Lord." The ideal land is not only covered in its whole extent with the atoning blood, but so deep is the stream that it buries all beneath it, except where upon the surface is displayed the significant inscription, "Holiness unto the Lord." Surely there is no lack in the provisions of salvation. "Where sin abounded, grace did much more abound: that as sin hath reigned unto death, even so might grace reign through righteousness unto eternal life, by Jesus Christ our Lord."

Thus, then, in these beautiful visions is it shown that the believer and the Church are sufficiently armed for the encounter with any antagonist, however furious or formidable. We are supplied with "the sword of the Spirit" and "the blood of the Lamb." Whatever the tasks may be that lie before us, having these, we have all necessary equipment. Nothing shall be able to harm us so long as we continue to be followers of God.

Revelation of Saint John

If the harvest scene illustrates the extent of divine grace, and is an emblem of the living seed which, small in its beginnings, grows into a great and widespreading tree under whose branches all the nations of earth may find shelter and rest, the vintage scene illustrates the depth to which salvation penetrates. The whole extent of human need is reached. Neither is there a want anywhere which may not be satisfied. And through the use of the divinely appointed means the kingdom of Christ may be brought to its ideal of perfection, in us and in the whole Church, until God shall, indeed, be all and in all.

PART V
The Counterfeit of the Kingdom, or the False Church

PART V

The Counterfeit of the Kingdom, or the False Church

THE section of the Revelation which we now reach, and which extends from chapter xv to the close of chapter xix, may be called the judgment section. There is a striking parallelism between it and part iii, or the vision of the trumpets, which symbolizes the methods through which the kingdom of Christ is furthered. As that section divided itself into two parts—first, the natural agencies which divine Providence employs, and, next, the supernatural word—so, also, this sets before us what may be designated natural judgments, and then those special visitations of divine justice which await an apostate Christian or Church.

1. *The Judgments of God. Vision of the Vials.*—The fifteenth and sixteenth chapters need not detain us long, inasmuch as the resemblance between them and the visions of the trumpets is so great that much of what might be said has already been anticipated. Vials, or basins rather, were vessels used in the Mosaic ritual as receptacles. The

term is used here to designate the judgments which must fall on men if the warnings and messages symbolized by the trumpets are unheeded. The Gospel, we are told by St. Paul, may be a savor of death unto death, as well as of life unto life. The words of the Lord Jesus will either become spirit and life to us, or they will judge us at the last day.

From "the temple of the tabernacle of the testimony" "seven angels" are seen issuing forth with vials containing "the seven last plagues." The word for "plague" is the same used in chapter xiii, 3. It was there applied to a temporary wound which was quickly healed. Its connection here with the word "last" and with the number "seven" indicates that the wounds or blows are final and incurable. The judgments are not corrective and disciplinary, but retributive and irreversible.

The angels with the plagues issue from the temple of the tabernacle of the testimony. This name is that which is applied to the structure Moses erected in the wilderness and which contained the ark of the testimony. Its use here implies that

The Counterfeit of the Kingdom

the judgments that follow are to be found recorded in the Old Testament Scriptures. The old word is God's faithful witness, bearing plain testimony to his righteousness and to his anger at sin and iniquity.

Still further, it was one of the four beasts, or living creatures, who put the vials into the hands of the angels; and, as the four beasts are supposed to be symbolical representations of the animate creation, the truth declared would seem to be that these judgments come as natural providences, or by the operation of laws which the divine Being has stamped on his creation.

The plagues fall successively upon the same places that are named in the parallel vision of the trumpets—the first upon the earth; the second, upon the sea; the third, upon the rivers and fountains of waters; the fourth, upon the sun; the fifth, upon the throne of the beast, darkening his kingdom; the sixth, upon the Euphrates.

It is very instructive to contrast these judgments with the beautiful figures by which John, in the last chapters of the Revelation, seeks to portray the glorious privileges and blessings of the perfected kingdom of Christ.

Thus, in opposition to the "noisome and grievous sore" that fell "upon the men which had the mark of the beast," we have, in chapter xxii, 2, the declaration that "the leaves of the tree" of life "were for the healing of the nations."

In opposition to "the sea" which "became as the blood of a dead man," we are told, in chapter xxi, 1, that "there was no more sea."

As a contrast to "the rivers and fountains of waters" which "became blood," we are told in chapter xxii, 1, of "the pure river of the water of life, clear as crystal."

Over against "the sun" which "scorched men with great heat," the statement is made, in chapter xxi, 23, that "the city had no need of the sun, neither of the moon, to shine in it: for the glory of God did lighten it, and the Lamb is the light thereof."

And, while judgment fell on the throne of the beast, "and his kingdom was full of darkness, and they gnawed their tongues for pain," we learn of the new city that "the throne of God and of the Lamb shall be in it; and his servants shall serve him." "And there shall be no night there; . . . for the Lord God giveth them light: and they shall reign forever and ever." There seems to be in this a reminiscence of the plague of darkness with which the Almighty visited Pharaoh and the Egyptians, and which was the last one before the final stroke of his judgment upon the firstborn (Exod. x, 21–23).

The fifth trumpet was interpreted as a prophecy of the blindness, both of heart and mind, which comes upon men when faith declines and grace wanes. This interpretation appears to be confirmed by the judgment which the plague of the fifth vial inflicts.

The locality of the sixth plague is the Euphrates. This river, as has been previously said, was the boundary line between civilization and barbarism. The mention of it implies that the last conflict in which the kingdom of Christ shall engage will be waged to oppose an inroad or outburst of barbarism. But as John presents this matter with fuller details in chapter xx the discussion of it will be postponed until that part of the Revelation is reached.

One new feature, which is introduced for the first time in connection with the sixth vial, is the singular sentence, "That the way of the kings of the east might be prepared." The origin of this expression is to be found in Isa. xli, 2, to which it has doubtless a reference. In that passage, "the righteous man from the east" to whom is given "rule over kings" is, undoubtedly, Cyrus, whose advent and success are thus foretold. And the meaning is that, as out of heathenism God raised up that marvelous man as an instrument to accomplish his purposes in the deliverance of his people, so there is such fullness of resources in the reach of divine power that in any emergency or peril he is able to find, anywhere, means to rescue his followers or his Church out of danger.

Moreover, the apostle saw coming "out of the mouth of the dragon, and out of the mouth of the beast, and out of the mouth of the false prophet" "three unclean spirits like frogs." Over against the divine Trinity, the kingdom of darkness and sin has its counterfeit trinity. Each of its component persons has its emissaries and messengers. For the final conflict all these will summon their entire resources. Behind all attempts to foil and defeat the development and perfection of the kingdom of Christ lie these evil powers. But their efforts will be futile; inevitable destruction and doom await them; and the inspired seer here merely suggests the judgment of which full particulars are to be subsequently given.

2. *Babylon and its Doom.*—No part of the Apocalypse has given rise to so much controversy as that which now engages our attention; and as, unhappily, the controversies have often originated in denominational prejudices and intensified denominational bitterness, this section has been made a shibboleth by which to test conflicting creeds. Truth is, indeed, of paramount obligation. We have no right to accept or reject interpretations of the Scriptures simply on the ground that they accord with or are repugnant to our beliefs. It is no part of our prerogative to sit in judgment upon the word of God or to force it to speak according to our mind. And nothing is ever really consistent with love which is not consistent with truth. If, however, the purpose of this remarkable book is to set before us those spiritual forces which work in the heart of every individual, as well as in collective masses, there seems no valid reason why we should in this part of it depart from those general principles upon which it is

elsewhere framed, or seek for latent meanings when one which lies on the surface is capable of explaining and harmonizing its mysteries.

Are we to understand by Babylon the Church of Rome, or the Roman Empire, or any specific body or association of men, religious or secular? Is the revelation here given us an anticipatory epitome of history, a foreshadowing of events that have already transpired and are now recorded among the annals of the race? Is it a prophecy the fulfillment of which can be known only by learned scholars acquainted with history, upon whose information the wayfaring man and the untutored disciple of Christ must depend? Is it a portion of Holy Writ whose best commentators must be found in Gibbon and Hume and such like unbelievers? Truly, then, Saul is "among the prophets;" and this book is singular and anomalous among the revelations of God, whose purpose has ever been to make wise the simple, who else would be cut off from access to the sources of truth and light.

If any of the prophecies of this book can be proven to find their exhaustive fulfillment in any particular and definite body,

The Counterfeit of the Kingdom

individual, or event, so that when we have identified the body or individual or event we have reached the whole purpose of the writer, then, of course, its value as inspiration ceases or, at least, is materially diminished. It may have an archæological interest as a record of past conditions, but its influence upon the present and future is somewhat like that of a fossil upon living types.

When the prophets of the old dispensation uttered their denunciations of the luxuries, the sensualism, the cruelty, the gilded vices, or the coarser sins of the cities and empires of the ancient world their purpose was not to vent vindictiveness against conquerors under whose might the Israel of God was oppressed and trampled down, but to direct thought and attention to a spirit of evil, a principle of the kingdom of darkness, which for a while found an embodiment therein, yet was not wholly comprehended in it. The empires crumbled into dust, the great capitals became masses of decaying ruins, but the spirit which animated them lived on, surviving their destruction.

Such was, doubtless, the design of this

Apocalyptic vision. Babylon is a symbol of something that has its fulfillment again and again, but is never exhausted in any manifestation. The generations of men, down to the close of time, must watch for and be warned against the spirit which it embodied, and every individual Christian, as well as the Church at large, needs the caution which is here given him against such forms of it as are likely to tempt him from the path of duty or safety.

Of all the hostile powers with which the Hebrew people were brought into contact and from whom they suffered Babylon seems to have been the most dreaded, and the animosity expressed toward it by the prophets was emphatic and marked. Its approaching doom evoked no sentiment of pity, but was hailed with unmingled satisfaction. What there was about Babylon which justified such exceptional fear and dislike it is, perhaps, not possible for us fully to understand, although we may attain some appreciation of it.

Regarding Nineveh, we have reason to conjecture that its peculiarity was intense and supreme secularism. No temple has been found amid its ruins that was not

The Counterfeit of the Kingdom

merely the adjunct of a palace. The priest was the servant of the king. All religious instincts and institutions were simply tools which the haughty monarch unscrupulously used to carry out his cruel and ambitious projects. Such a condition of things can never endure long. It works its own destruction, finding its cure within itself. It was the demoralization resulting from a similar condition which sapped the strength of the Greek Empire of Byzantium and, by isolating it from all allies or sympathy, led to its overthrow.

In Egypt the spheres of the State and of the Church maintained some independence of each other. Vast as was the sovereignty of the Pharaohs, it was not such as to encroach upon or absorb the functions of the priestly caste.

In Babylon, however, still another condition prevailed. Here the priesthood was the ruling order; the religious element dominated the secular. The palace was a part of the temple. It is noticeable how strongly in the prophetic descriptions of Babylon the Chaldean element is emphasized. It is styled "the beauty of the Chaldees' excellency," "the land of the

Chaldeans," marking thus the supremacy of that order of soothsayers, sorcerers, and professors of magic and occult science. Babylon was a theocracy, but the god who ruled it was the prince of darkness, not Jehovah. The Church governed the State, but the Church was one that incarnated the spirit of worldly-mindedness, not heavenly-mindedness. So that, in an altogether peculiar and special sense, it was the rival and counterfeit of the true Church of God, giving exercise to the religious instincts of men sufficient to satisfy conviction and quiet conscience, while debasing them by turning them into the channels of lust and sensual gratification.

Yet, as a matter of fact, the domination of Babylon proved less hurtful to the Jewish nation than did the hostility of any other of their great enemies. The form of worldliness which the Israelites encountered in Egypt was such as almost to make them forget their bondage in remembering the enjoyments they had found there. Their actual experience in Babylon during the years of their captivity, the lessons they learned and the comparisons they drew when brought into personal relationship

The Counterfeit of the Kingdom

with its life, left no lingering love of idolatry and cured them forever of any desire to worship its gods.

But the Babylon of the book of Revelation comprehends more than the Babylon of the Hebrew prophets. The dangers which beset the Christian would be far less than they are if the Babylon of this world, which opposes itself as a rival to the kingdom of Christ, had no fascinations beyond those which the great city by the Euphrates could offer. The wily enemy of mankind is too subtle to depend upon any such powers of attractiveness as were embodied in the capital of the Chaldean Empire. And in describing the counterfeit of the kingdom of Christ the writer of the Apocalypse adds to his portrait of Babylon features which are used by Ezekiel as characteristic of another great capital, Tyre. Babylon was never a center of commerce; in no sense could it be described as a city whose merchants were princes. The same is also true of Rome, and is thus adverse to the opinion that John meant to describe the city of the Cæsars and of the popes. His delineation of Babylon would apply to Corinth or Carthage in ancient times, and to Venice or

Amsterdam or London in more modern days, with greater aptness than to the metropolis on the Tiber. In this alteration of the emblem in which the writer of the Revelation indulges, in the blending and interweaving of details descriptive of both the Babylon and the Tyre of the Old Testament into the composite figure of the Apocalyptic Babylon, in the transition from Isaiah's sublimely ironical shout of triumph over the metropolis by the Euphrates to Ezekiel's sad and pathetic dirge over the fall of the commercial emporium of Phœnicia, a clew is given us to the interpretation of his meaning.

The influence of Tyre upon the Hebrew people and religion was always deleterious, almost disastrous. The intercourse which began in the magnificent Solomon's love of show and splendid state and luxury, and which was increased by the intermarriage of the royal houses of Ahab and Jehoshaphat with Tyrian princesses, was fruitful of moral degeneration. From the spiritual pesthouse upon the Mediterranean came, first, Tyrian art, then, Tyrian wares, then, Tyrian idols, and, then, the unbridled and lawless sensualities for which Tyre was noto-

The Counterfeit of the Kingdom

rious, until Baal had displaced the golden calves set up by Jeroboam in Bethel and had well-nigh overthrown the altars of Jehovah in the city of the great King.

The Babylon which John saw and whose rise and fall he predicts was one that embraced in itself the unbounded pride, the self-sufficingness, the love of sorceries and dark arts of magic, along with the demoralizing practices of a great mart of commerce —a mongrel figure into which all forms of evil and sin were woven.

The probability, therefore, is that John meant to describe, not any individual or definite city or Church, but the incarnation of a spurious and apostate Christianity which, assuming the appearance of the true, is animated by principles wholly destitute of and antagonistic to the power and life of Christianity, and thus deludes only to destroy.

This opinion derives confirmation from the connection in which the section stands. Up to this point the writer of the Revelation has been collecting his data, so to speak, summing up the elementary forces, friendly and hostile, which have to do with the success or failure of the kingdom of

Christ. He has announced its fundamental principles, the means by which it is to be carried forward, the enemies which must be encountered. It now remains for him to show in a concrete form the results. At the close of the Revelation he shows us the result of success in that exquisite picture of the ideal true Christianity. But before doing this he also shows the result of failure in the picture of the ideal false Christianity. The antitheses between the two are drawn out in sharp contrasts.

In chapter xxi, 9, it is said to him, "Come hither, I will show thee the bride, the Lamb's wife." Here (xvii, 1) it is said to him, "Come hither: I will show unto thee the judgment of the great whore that sitteth upon many waters."

In chapter xxi, 6, it is written, "He said unto me, It is done." So here (chapter xvi, 17), when the seventh angel poured out his vial a voice was heard crying, "It is done."

In chapter xii, where for the first time the field of battle is described and the enumeration of the hostile forces is begun, religion is presented to us under the figure of a woman who has fled to the wilderness. Since then the trial is supposed to have been gone through with, the long war has been fought, the varying moments of the struggle have been detailed, and we are now brought to the summing up of the issue.

In chapter xxi, 10, John is carried away "in the spirit to a great and high mountain," and there is shown him the woman in the form of "that great city," "the holy city, new Jerusalem, coming down from God out of heaven, prepared as a bride adorned for her husband" (verse 2). Here (xvii, 3, 4) he is carried away "in the spirit into the wilderness," and he sees the woman; but now she is sitting "upon a scarlet-colored beast, full of names of blasphemy, . . . arrayed in purple and scarlet color, and decked with gold." She has failed in the conflict. She has not come victorious out of the wilderness, as Christ did after his temptation. She has made peace with her enemies. She has joined with the flesh, the world, and the devil. She is no longer spotless and pure, ready for her bridal with the Lamb, but has become a harlot.

Thus, once, Orpah and Ruth stood together by the side of Naomi, while the Holy Land beckoned them all toward it.

Ruth chose that better part and, sheltered beneath the hovering wings of the God of Israel, found peace and rest and an eternal portion with the saints; but Orpah loved the blue hills of Moab and, though sadly and reluctantly, turned back to idolatry and oblivion and spiritual death.

Such a conflict awaits us all; and the issue must be, either that happy one hereafter to be more accurately described under the figure of the New Jerusalem, or else that alliance with the powers of darkness which John records in the emblem of Babylon.

The details of the description given of Babylon add further confirmation to the explanation offered above. In chapters xii and xiii the three great enemies of the kingdom of Christ were enumerated—the dragon and his emissaries, the two beasts. In the present chapter (xvii) they are represented as combined. The woman is seen sitting upon a scarlet-colored beast. She is arrayed in purple and scarlet, but not in "fine linen," which is "the righteousness of saints." She has in her hand a cup, but instead of the sacramental blood of the Lamb, it is full of "abominations and filthiness of her fornication." She is not "filled

The Counterfeit of the Kingdom

with the Spirit," but "drunken with the blood of the saints," for "she hath cast down many wounded, yea, many strong men have been slain by her" (Prov. vii, 26).

It will be remembered that, in the description of the first wild beast, it is said that when the deadly wound which it had received was healed the whole world wondered after it in astonishment at the recuperative power which it exhibited. But, at this vision of the woman allied with the beast, with a commingling of the influence of the second wild beast, even John himself wondered with great wonder at a corruption of religion so complete and yet so enticing, a perversion so unexpected and yet so alluring, a transformation so plausibly and artfully accomplished. There seems to have been awakened in him something of the perplexity he had experienced in looking at the second wild beast, as if its duplicity were a mystery of iniquity beyond his power to fathom. Once one of the psalmists wondered, as he tells us, at the prosperity of the wicked, until he entered the sanctuary and there saw their latter end foreshadowed. So, likewise, was the mind of John relieved by the angel who came to him and said, "I will tell thee the mystery of the woman, and of the beast that carrieth her;" for as the curtain was lifted the doom of Babylon was revealed to him and the mystery was solved.

But, however plain the mystery was to him, it is assuredly not equally so to us. The explanation which suggests itself to us the most readily is not necessarily the most correct one; indeed, the words, "Here is the mind which hath wisdom," seem to indicate otherwise and to force us to seek some meaning deeper than that which is most obvious. Although, therefore, the expression, "The seven heads are seven mountains, on which the woman sitteth," apparently identifies Babylon with Rome, either imperial or papal, it would satisfy all the conditions of the problem as well, and be more in harmony with the principles on which the Revelation is constructed, to interpret the expression as referring to the great world empires which have successively dominated the human race and cast their shadows across the path of centuries, and in which John saw the embodiment of the world-principle, essentially and perpetually antagonistic to the kingdom of Christ.

The Counterfeit of the Kingdom

Of these world empires five had already fallen—Assyria, Babylon, Persia, Macedonia, and the empire of Alexander's successors. The empire of Rome, which was the one existent in John's days and the most compact and formidable of them all, was the sixth. "The other," he says, "is not yet come; and when he cometh, he must continue a short space." Of this difficult passage many explanations have been offered, but it cannot be said that they are satisfactory. Whether John anticipated the fall of the Roman Empire and the establishment of another world empire to succeed it for a brief period of time we are not able to say.

It would not be any impeachment of the inspiration of the apostles to admit that upon matters relating to the time of our Lord's coming they were not able to predict with certainty. Christ himself said that "of that day and hour knoweth no man, no, not the angels which are in heaven, neither the Son, but the Father;" and we cannot concede that his disciples were more fully enlightened than he. There are indications that the apostles anticipated the personal manifestation of the Master at a date earlier than has proven to be the fact, because, looking through the ages, mountains appeared in their vision to blend into one which we have found by experience to be separated by valleys deep and wide.

But, inasmuch as it was revealed to John that prior to the realization of the ideal kingdom of Christ there is to be a decisive conflict with the combined powers of evil, as will be more fully discussed when we shall have reached the twentieth chapter of the book, may it not be that it is that final embodiment of the world-principle which he here foretells as the seventh antagonistic kingdom?

"And the beast that was, and is not, even he is the eighth, and is of the seven, and goeth into perdition." These words seem to imply that this "eighth" is not a separate and distinct empire, but is that common principle of worldliness which finds its embodiment in all the seven and yet is distinct and separable from them. It is both immanent in them and transcendental to them.

And there is, perhaps, here an intended and striking contrast between this evil principle and the divine Being with whom it

The Counterfeit of the Kingdom

assumes to contest supremacy. It was said of the Lord God Almighty, in the adoration of the living creatures (Rev. iv, 8), that he "was, and is, and is to come." Of this counterfeit principle of evil it must be said, "It was, and is not." God is true, real, the same to-day as yesterday and forever. He that hath received Christ's testimony can set his seal to this assured and blessed certainty. Of the evil principle it can only be said that it is always vanity, falsehood, a lie. Its past is all a bitter remembrance; its future a shadow, a deception, a dream; and he that trusts it is a fool mocked with illusions that are never realized and cheated with hopes that forever disappoint.

It is not likely that any world-kingdom comparable in extent and power with those which in ancient times subjugated mankind will ever be seen again. Christianity develops and cultivates a spirit of individualism which is inimical to their recurrence. Since the disappearance of the Roman Empire no successor to it has arisen. The empires of Charlemagne and Napoleon were narrow and petty in comparison with that of the Cæsars. Some such thought appears to have been in the mind of John when he foretold that there shall be "ten kings, which have received no kingdom as yet; but receive power as kings one hour with the beast."

But the spirit of evil which finds temporary embodiment in these worldly sovereignties does not disappear with their overthrow. It incarnates itself in other and more dangerous forms. There are subtle and cunning manifestations of this spirit which, by plausible and enticing imitations of the religion of Christ, do far more than any worldly kingdom can to overthrow true Christianity and substitute in its place the counterfeit kingdom, the deadly rival which is designated by the emblem of Babylon.

Without violating the spirit of charity, and in fealty to the obligation of truth, it must be confessed that the history of the Church of Rome has too often furnished just occasion for its identification with the Babylon of the Apocalypse. Its worldliness, its unscrupulous alliances with kings and princes to carry out its ambitious projects, its disregard of moral obligations in the pursuit of its policy, its ignoring of the

The Counterfeit of the Kingdom

demands of justice, honor, truth and mercy, its persistent struggle to achieve and maintain temporal supremacy, its awful claim of present and eternal mastery over the bodies, minds, and souls of men, its luxury and wantonness, its bloody spirit of persecution on the one hand, and, on the other, the duplicity, the false asceticism, the assumption of the appearance of the Lamb while animated by the spirit of the dragon, the substitution of its own codes and edicts and ethics for the word of God, which have specially characterized its religious orders and confraternities, are sufficiently like the adversary of true religion delineated by St. John to excite thought and induce self-examination.

But it would be unjust to charge to the account of systems imperfections and errors which spring out of the inherent frailty of human nature. And the spirit of evil against which the apostle warns us has had unhappily a range wider than pagan or papal Rome or any organization yet witnessed on earth. If that Church has too often carried upon her forehead the title, "Mother of harlots," instead of the motto, "Holiness unto the Lord," she has many a sister who must sit beside her as of kindred spirit; and, if the one has been "Aholah," the other has been "Aholibah." If, among her followers, she has numbered both some of the purest saints who have trodden this earth and some of the vilest sinners, and these, too, in her loftiest places, she is not alone in the distinction.

There have been individuals and Churches calling themselves Christians and Protestants that, like veritable Messalinas, have burned with incessant lust after every form and fashion of worldliness, and whose lovers, as Jeremiah says, have not had need to weary themselves in seeking for them. There is too much truth in the biting sarcasm of Heine: "Christianity was once based on blood; it now rests on another basis—money. Wafers of silver and gold are the only ones that work miracles in modern days." When the solemn services of the holy sacraments lose their attraction and are accounted dull and pale when compared with the brighter light of social festivities; when prayer meetings are sparsely attended, while glittering parlors are crowded with guests; when the shouting of souls newly born into the kingdom is

The Counterfeit of the Kingdom

drowned by the "chant to the sound of the viol;" when grief over "the affliction of Joseph" is far less than the sorrow for the loss of worldly prestige or patronage; when religion is used simply as an adjunct to the social propensities or a synonym for liberality in promoting financial enterprises—then there is need that we read again the apocalyptic vision of Babylon, that we may avert the doom that is certain otherwise to come. Destruction must surely be the end of those "whose god is their belly, and whose glory is their shame, who mind earthly things." The vials of divine anger must sooner or later empty their plagues upon all such.

In the selection and introduction of Tyre as the representative of a worldly Church the apostle indicates the source from which danger is to be apprehended. Tyre was a mart of commerce. Upon her ships the merchandise of the world was transported, and it was sold in her markets. Her trade extended to the ends of the earth, and by her mercantile transactions she was brought into contact with the whole circle of known nations. The close acquaintance and fellowship thereby wrought with all religions, races, and customs produced its customary result of lowering the standard of morals and, under the specious plea of encouraging liberalism of opinion, led to apathy toward all religion; while, at the same time, the increase of wealth, art, and refinement created a love for luxury and worldly good. Corrupted herself, she became in turn a source of corruption to others, and her intercourse with Israel had a disastrous effect upon the chosen people.

In this lies the peril of contact with the world. It is the scene of conflict; it may be the field either of defeat or victory. The Lord Jesus prayed, not that his disciples should be taken out of the world, but that they should be preserved from its evil. We are placed in it that we may transform it. It is possible that all beauty, art, wealth, culture, and commerce may be sanctified and made to contribute to the redemption of the world. Every thought may be brought into captivity to the obedience of Christ.

But it may, on the contrary, transform and corrupt us. Without the aid of supernatural grace the influence of the world upon the Christian is demoralizing and destructive.

The Counterfeit of the Kingdom

Whatever is without God is equally without hope. Art, for instance, separated from its mission as an auxiliary to morals and religion and made independent, becomes artificial, and then degenerates into artifice. The world, instead of being lifted to a higher plane, drags the Christian to its own level. It is remarkable that Paul, whose facilities of observation were large and powers of perception keen, when writing to the Romans, the people of the eternal city, whose one dream and ambition in all her history had been power, commended the Gospel of Christ as "the power of God unto salvation;" but, when writing to Corinth, the busy center of commerce and merchandise, full of wealth, luxury, and corruption, he presented as the only influence which could correct these evils this profound truth: "Know ye not that ye are not your own? For ye are bought with a price: therefore glorify God."

There has not been a period since the days of John when the lesson which he wished to enforce in this vision of apostate and fallen Babylon was more important than now. Between the age of the apostles and the times in which we live a stronger resemblance exists than between any epochs in the annals of man. The rapid increase of means of transportation by which the ends of the earth are drawn together is effecting that state of things which the consolidation of the civilized world under the control of the Roman Empire produced. The boundaries between nations are being effaced; and their easy communication with each other makes possible an exceptional intermingling of languages, usages, moral codes, and religion. There is the same tendency toward the denial of all supernaturalism, on one side, and, at the opposite extreme, toward an eclecticism which concedes some truth to all forms of religion, while questioning the absolute truth of any, as that with which the apostolic Church was confronted. There is an excessive liberalism which, in its aversion to narrowness and under the plea of enlightened culture, would abandon all that specifically differentiates Christianity. But we will have read the records of the ante-Nicene period in vain if we have not learned from them that an imperfect Christianity, while it does not gain the world, does lose its own soul, and that the regeneration of mankind keeps

The Counterfeit of the Kingdom

exact pace with the measure of spirituality and purity which prevails in the Church of Christ.

Babylon, the counterfeit of the kingdom, is doomed to inevitable destruction. Over the sad end of a Church dominated by the spirit of the world and which has finally apostatized from Christ the worldly may say, in regretful lament, "Alas, alas, that great city;" the "merchants of the earth" may "weep and mourn over her; for no man buyeth their merchandise any more;" but the heavens rejoice. For where there is permanent alienation from God no real life can survive: "The voice of the bridegroom and of the bride shall be heard no more at all in thee." There can be no fruitful activity or profitable labor, for "the sound of a millstone shall be heard no more at all in thee." There can be no inward illumination or safe walking, for "the light of a candle shall shine no more at all in thee."

3. *Methods of Success Reiterated.*—After a few words of exultant triumph over the fall of Babylon, and the bright hopes for the future of Christ's kingdom opened up thereby, in which heaven and earth unite, the apostle, before finally leaving the sub-

ject, points us again (in chapter xix) to the weapons by which victory must be won. Repeating what has been so often said by him that the impression is made on us that herein lies the central thought of the book, but with a fullness of detail not previously equaled and with a stress of emphasis which guarantees the importance of the truth, he asserts again that the conquering weapons are "the blood of the Lamb" and "the word of their testimony" (Rev. xii, 11; xix, 15). The cross and the Bible—these are the means by which the world is to be overcome, these are the instruments through which the Lord Jesus Christ and the Holy Ghost work, and with these the Christian and the Church are sufficiently armed for any conflict or adversary.

John saw "heaven opened (verse 11), and behold a white horse." Thus does the Christ appear at the close of the conflict, sitting upon the white horse of victory, just as he appeared at the beginning when, armed with the bow, "he went forth conquering, and to conquer" (chap. vi, 2). He is described by the titles which he had attributed to himself in his letters to the seven churches of Asia. He is here the "Faithful

The Counterfeit of the Kingdom

and True;" so had he written of himself to Laodicea. "In righteousness he doth judge and make war;" to Philadelphia he had called himself "he that is holy, he that is true." "His eyes were as a flame of fire;" these very words he had written to Thyatira. "Out of his mouth proceedeth a sharp sword;" to Pergamos he had spoken of himself as the one having "the sharp sword." To Ephesus he had described himself as the one that "walketh in the midst of the golden candlesticks [or churches];" and here he is seen in company with the armies of his followers. He had promised Sardis that the faithful should walk with him "in white;" here the saints with him are "clothed in fine linen, white and clean." To Smyrna he had said, "I will give thee a crown of life;" and here upon his head are "many crowns." He has a name which all can read, "King of kings, and Lord of lords," ruling (shepherding) the nations with the iron staff of his power. But he has also a name that no man knoweth; for he had himself said, "No man knoweth the Son, but the Father." He is the Word of God, the embodiment and utterance of the Godhead's deepest thought and being, the "brightness" of the Father's glory, "and the express image of his person."

The weapons which he employs are distinctly said to be the "sharp sword" that goeth "out of his mouth," and the blood by which he atoned for sin. The "sharp sword" means, unquestionably, "the sword of the Spirit," the word inspired by the Spirit of truth, the Scriptures which testify of him (John v, 39), the word by which we are sanctified (John xvii, 17), the Bible of revelation. By this word, "the breath of his lips," he slays the wicked (Isa. xi, 4). With this, "the spirit of his mouth," he consumes the wicked one (2 Thess. ii, 8).

And the other weapon is his blood. He is "clothed with a vesture dipped in blood." "He treadeth the wine press of the fierceness and wrath of Almighty God." In no way could the cross be more explicitly indicated. Lifted up from the earth upon it, he draws all men unto himself. It is "Christ crucified" who is the "power" and "wisdom" of God. No weapons more carnal than these does he employ; none other do we need. By them the beast and the false prophet are overcome, and both are "cast alive into a lake of fire."

PART VI

Progressive Steps by Which the Ideal Kingdom of Christ is to be Realized

PART VI

Progressive Steps by Which the Ideal Kingdom of Christ is to be Realized

THE twentieth chapter of the Revelation is one full of the most important matter. It describes the stages through which the kingdom of Christ must pass in order to attain its ideal state. The key to its solution is to be found in a careful and close study of the prophecy of Ezekiel, between which and it so exact a parallelism exists that neither can be understood without a comprehension of the other. A just appreciation of this fact would have precluded many of the ingenious but untenable hypotheses which have based themselves upon this section, and will now serve to throw light upon what seems obscure and almost undecipherable.

The Book of Ezekiel consists of two distinct parts, the dividing line between which is the siege and capture of Jerusalem. The earlier part of the book is a record of the many and gross idolatries and sins into which Israel had been tempted and fallen. The sum of these amounted to a spiritual infidelity and adultery which justly deserved the anger of Jehovah. And it was the sad and painful task of the prophet to repeat the solemn warnings with which he had been intrusted of impending and terrible doom.

Succeeding this are denunciations by the prophet of severe and crushing judgments upon the surrounding nations, from whose intercourse Israel has received deadly harm, being corrupted by contact with them, both in peace and war, and more especially in a lowered spiritual life. This part of the Book of Ezekiel comes to an end in chapter xxxiii, 21, where the mournful announcement is made to the prophet that the predicted blow had fallen: "One that had escaped out of Jerusalem came to me, saying, The city is smitten." It was a conclusive proof of his authority to be considered a true prophet of God, but not less deplorable on that account.

The remaining part of the book is taken up with brighter themes. Out of the nettle, danger, God has plucked the flower, safety. The fall of Jerusalem, which seemed to involve its disappearance from history, is the means of its salvation. The pages of the prophet are bright with his predictions of an Israel raised to a new and higher ideal, and restored thereby to the favor of God. The steps by which this happy condition is to be brought about are successively unfolded to us and occupy the book to its close. The false shepherds (chapter xxxiv), the unworthy and unfaithful rulers who, like the thieves and hirelings of whom Jesus spake (John x), fed themselves and cared naught for the flock, are to be removed; and God offers himself to be a shepherd to Israel, searching his sheep, seeking them out in the cloudy and dark day, binding up that which was broken, and bringing again that which was lost—a beautiful predictive type of the Messiah, the good Shepherd who laid down his life for the sheep.

In addition to this, the false prophets and unsafe guides whom Israel had followed are to be taken out of the way, and God promises in their stead to put his Spirit within Israel, cleansing them from all their filthiness and their idols and giving them a new heart and a new spirit (xxxvi, 25–27). This promise of spiritual regeneration is illustrated by the vision of the valley of dry bones (xxxvii, 1–14). At the word of the prophet "the bones" which lay whitening in the valley "came together, bone to his bone," assuming the form and appearing in the likeness of men. But something more than human preaching was required, for as yet the forms were without life. Then the "breath" of the Holy Spirit entered into them, like the wind whose sound was heard on the day of Pentecost, "and they lived, and stood up upon their feet, an exceeding great army" of actual and real men.

The first and closely following result of the spiritual resurrection thus wrought by the Holy Spirit was the reunion of Judah and Ephraim (verses 15-28). These two branches of Israel, unhappily disunited, always suspicious of each other, often in actual hostility, had by their division brought reproach upon God's cause and had subjected themselves to the disasters, oppressions, and captivities which had marked their history. Now the schism was to be healed. They were to become one, so that God could say again, "They shall be my people, and I will be their God." Then shall follow a new era of unexampled peace, prosperity, and productiveness. "David my servant shall be king over them," "their prince forever." "My tabernacle also shall be with them; yea, I will be their

God, and they shall be my people. And the heathen shall know that I the Lord do sanctify Israel." The fulfillment of part of this prophecy is distinctly declared by the angel of God who announced to the Virgin Mary concerning Christ (Luke i, 32), "The Lord God shall give unto him the throne of his father David: and he shall reign over the house of Jacob forever; and of his kingdom there shall be no end." Now it is a remarkable fact, of which use will hereafter be made to clear up the mystery of one of the obscurest parts of the Revelation of John, that the reign of David and his descendants over the throne of Jerusalem was exactly one thousand years. In the year 1063 B. C. David was anointed king by Samuel and won his first triumph in his memorable overthrow of Goliath; and in 63 B. C. Judea became subject to Rome, and the royal supremacy of David's line came to an end.* The "scepter" then departed from Judah, and the "lawgiver from between his feet."

Immediately following this remarkable prophecy of Ezekiel is that concerning "Gog, the land of Magog" (chapters xxxviii, xxxix). He is instructed to say

---

* Dr. William Smith, *New Testament History*, p. 731.

to Gog, "After many days thou shalt be visited: in the latter years thou shalt come into the land that is brought back from the sword" (xxxviii, 8); "Thou shalt ascend and come like a storm" (xxxviii, 9); "Thou shalt come up against my people of Israel" (xxxviii, 16); nevertheless, in the thirty-ninth chapter it is recorded, "I am against thee, O Gog" (xxxix, 1); "Thou shalt fall upon the mountains of Israel, thou, and all thy bands, and the people that is with thee: I will give thee unto the ravenous birds of every sort, and to the beasts of the field to be devoured" (xxxix, 4); "Then shall they [that is, Israel] know that I am the Lord their God" (xxxix, 28); "Neither will I hide my face any more from them: for I have poured out my Spirit upon the house of Israel, saith the Lord God" (xxxix, 29).

Ezekiel closes his prophecies (chapters xl–xlviii) with his pictures of restored Israel, its new ideal temple, and city, and land.

The lines of thought thus laid down by the prophet of the Old Testament are so closely followed by the author of the Apocalypse that there seems no other conclusion left to us than that the parallelism of subject is intended to be as exact as is that of language and imagery.

In the Apocalypse, too, "the faithful city" (Isa. i, 21) has forfeited her faith and "become an harlot." The dire catastrophe which the seer of the old dispensation saw falling upon corrupt and apostate Jerusalem has also fallen upon Babylon, the unfaithful Church of the new. So, also, before the eyes of the apostle, as well as those of the prophet, there gleamed a vision of a restored Church, pure and clean, descending from God out of heaven, adorned as a bride for her husband. How this vision is to be made real, how that splendid city is to be brought into existence of whose glories the eloquent figures of the closing chapters inspire such lofty conceptions, it remains for him to tell us, in order that in all ages to come Christian men may discern the paths along which they must labor and the steps through which they must ascend if their efforts are to be crowned with favor and success.

How valuable a help the study of Ezekiel affords us in the interpretation of the Apocalypse may be seen in the light which it throws upon the subject of the "thousand years." The foundation of those theories of a millennium which have taken such hold upon the minds of men as to have perceptibly modified language and to have made the word one of the commonplaces of thought lies in the few verses which make up the first half of the twentieth chapter. There must be something peculiarly attractive about these theories and very much in them accordant with our instinctive hopes, since the paragraph in the text furnishes but a narrow basis upon which to build a superstructure so large. It is not easy, moreover, to understand why, in a book so allegorical as is the Apocalypse, this paragraph should enjoy the exceptional distinction of demanding a literal interpretation, as would be the case if these theories are admitted. Nevertheless, it is true that, from very early ages in Christian history until now, a belief in and expectation of a personal and visible appearance and reign upon earth of the Lord Jesus Christ, inaugurating with his saints a period, stretching through a thousand years, of inconceivable peace and prosperity, has been entertained by many of his purest and most zealous followers, and has even been made the distinguishing tenet of large bodies of men.

Progressive Steps

Whether these opinions are legitimately based upon the text and how far a correct exegesis compels us to accept them we must now inquire, endeavoring in all fairness and candor to so interpret the inspired words as to make the various details of the paragraph consistent with each other and with the rest of the sacred Scriptures.

Referring once more to the prophecy of Ezekiel, we find the order of events there described to be, first, a resurrection of dry bones and a vivification of them into men, then a united Church and people of God, an undefined period of happy prosperity, a restoration of the kingdom of David, a combined assault upon this kingdom by hostile nations under the name of Gog and Magog, and the complete and final victory of the kingdom over them.

In the Apocalypse the same order is followed, with variation only in some details of the picture. The only feature which can be called new is that of the binding and loosing of Satan; and even this, by implication, at least, is in Ezekiel. It is certainly a reasonable presumption that the same truths, whatever they are, were in the mind both of the prophet and the apostle, and were intended to be taught by both.

Now, if anything in the interpretation of the Apocalypse may be relied on as valid and beyond question it is that the reign of Christ is not a future event, to be expected at some day which has not yet dawned upon earth, but is a present and existent fact. That kingdom was inaugurated when the Lord Jesus, having risen from the dead and ascended to heaven, led captivity captive and bestowed upon his followers the gift of the Holy Spirit. When St. Paul in writing to the Corinthians says, "He must reign, till he hath put all enemies under his feet," surely the meaning is that he does now reign and shall continue so to do until the result is accomplished.

The mediatorial sovereignty of the Lord Jesus Christ is, indeed, the one theme of the whole book of Revelation. The consummation and undisputed supremacy of the kingdom has not been reached. It is in its militant, not triumphant state. But imperfection within and hostility without no more affect the reality of its being, although they may militate against its well-being, than did treason within and war without contravene the fact of the sovereignty of David and his house over Judah. Into this kingdom not a select number, but all the true followers of Jesus are introduced. They are "a royal priesthood." They are "joint heirs with Christ." "We see not yet," indeed, "all things put under him;" but we see Jesus "crowned with glory and honor;" and "he that sanctifieth and they who are sanctified are all of one: for which cause he is not ashamed to call them brethren."

Again, it may be accepted as almost an axiom of interpretation that the resurrection referred to in the words, "They lived and reigned with Christ," means a spiritual change, and not a physical or bodily one. It is synonymous with that epoch in the Christian's life when he is delivered "from the power of darkness" and translated "into the kingdom of God's dear Son," that crisis of spiritual existence which is called conversion or regeneration, when one is "born from above" and raised with Christ into newness of life. The resurrection spoken of is stated to be that of "the souls of them that were beheaded for the witness of Jesus, and for the word of God, and which had not worshiped the beast, neither his image." It is also called "the first resurrection," thus differentiating it from another and subsequent resurrection of "the rest of the dead." This first resurrection, moreover, exempts those who partake of it from the power of "the second death," which is defined as the being "cast into the lake of fire." It separates them from "the rest of the dead"—those who are dead "in trespasses and sins," as they themselves once were—who live not again until "the thousand years" are finished.

We are now on sure ground. The meaning of this vision is that the mediatorial kingdom of our Lord is to be established on the earth, and that by the proper use of those instrumentalities which have been given into our hands, namely, the word of God and the blood of the Lamb, it shall advance in spite of all opposition and hindrances, until all worldliness and false prophetism shall be eliminated, until Christ "shall have put down all rule and all authority and power," until "the kingdoms of this world" shall become "the kingdoms of our Lord, and of his Christ," and "he shall have delivered up the kingdom to God, even the Father," and the prayer shall be fulfilled which daily ascends to the throne of grace, " Thy kingdom come." The millennium is now. We are living in it. Its light shines but dimly, it is true, but it will shine more and more until the perfect day.

The period during which the saints shall live and reign with Christ is stated to be "a thousand years." Conjecture has been rife as to why this number should be selected. Manifestly, here, at least, the year-day theory, that which makes every day mentioned in the book the symbol of a year, breaks down. Otherwise, the period would be too long; and none have been found to maintain the opinion that the millennium is to last three hundred and sixty-five thousand years. Yet, to interpret the expression literally, as if it meant exactly a thousand of our years, would be to depart entirely from the rule of the Apocalypse, in which numbers are taken as symbols of epochs, not as a measurement of duration. There is no reason given why in this case exception should be made to the constant and unvarying use of days and months and years in this book.

Here, again, reference to the book of Ezekiel will dissolve the obscurity and present us with an explanation simple, consistent, and entirely in accordance with the usage which elsewhere prevails in the Apocalypse.

In the description which Ezekiel gives of the happy results which were to follow the resurrection of the dry bones and the reunion of Israel, one of the particulars which tenderly touched every Jewish heart was, "David my servant shall be king over them; and they shall all have one shepherd." Whether the prophet was himself conscious of the full meaning of these words or not, it is nevertheless the fact that it was not in any merely earthly descendant of David that this prediction was to be realized, but in the Messiah, "great David's greater Son." So, doubtless, the apostle of the Apocalypse accepted it. And, inasmuch as the sovereignty of David's house was, as has previously been said, just one thousand years, what more natural than that John should see in this number the signature and symbol of the reign of Christ? He does not mean that the duration of that reign shall be limited to a thousand years, but that, be it longer or shorter, this number is its symbol and emblem. Whatever he mentions as taking place during the thousand years is to be understood by us as occurring during the progress of the mediatorial kingdom of Christ from its commencement to its culmination. In the sight of the divine Being the period between the establishment of the kingdom and its complete and final triumph over all its foes, be it longer or shorter, is the day of Christ, and "one day is with the Lord as a thousand years, and a thousand years as one day."

The moments or stages in the growth of the kingdom are now to be specified.

1. *Restraints upon the Power of Satan.*—There is one item in the revelation made to John, and through him to us, which is peculiar to him. It is, indeed, implied in the book of Ezekiel, but is not explicitly communicated. This is the restraint which is put upon the power of Satan. An angel is seen to " come down from heaven, having the key of the bottomless pit [the same mentioned in chapter ix, 1–11] and a great chain in his hand [see 2 Pet. ii, 4; Jude 6]. And he laid hold on the dragon, that old serpent, which is the Devil, and Satan, and

bound him a thousand years." "When the thousand years are expired, Satan shall be loosed out of his prison, and shall go out to deceive the nations;" but this loosing of him, it is said, will be for only "a little season" before his final destruction. As the thousand years are a synonym for the reign of Christ, the meaning is that during the existent mediatorial sovereignty of Christ Satan is debarred his full liberty. His judgment has not, indeed, come, and he still exists, but his activity is circumscribed, and his power to hurt is limited and curbed.

It will be remembered that in the twelfth chapter Satan was described under the emblem of the dragon and his futile hostility toward the woman was depicted. At the close of the chapter we were told that "the dragon was wroth with the woman, and went to make war with the remnant of her seed." Since that time he has seemed to disappear from mention and is directly alluded to only occasionally. His place in the drama of warfare has been taken by the two wild beasts, his emissaries, in whom all enmity against Christ and his followers has been concentrated. Now that these have been judged and consigned to their doom and have in turn passed from the stage, the apostle reverts to the evil one behind and within them, whose subordinate agents they were.

One of the noteworthy facts of the universe brought to light mainly by this book of Revelation, but fully corroborated by other scriptures when attention is directed to its quest, is the ambition of Satan to copy and travesty the divine Being, both in modes of manifestation and methods of work. His abilities seem to lie, not in the direction of originality, but of imitation. He is not a creator or inventor, but a consummate actor and a master of the art of mimicry. As the Deity is revealed to us in the triune personality of Father, Son, and Spirit, so also there is a trinity of evil—the dragon, the beast, and the false prophet.

And, again, during the continuance of the mediatorial sovereignty of Christ established for the elimination of sin from the universe the Father does not directly interpose, but has delivered all things into the hands of the Son, and through him to the Holy Spirit, whose instruments are the cross and the Bible, and whose witnesses and memorials are the two sacraments. In like manner, there is an attempted imitation of this on the part of Satan. His personal agency in human affairs is confined within narrow limits, not of his own will surely, but by reason of him who hath subjected him. Whatever influence his malignity and deep-seated hatred of God can exert in order to defeat the plans and purposes of redemption is wielded mainly through his subordinates, the two wild beasts. He himself is incarcerated in the abyss of darkness at the will of his Master and Lord. He seems to have been allowed personally to tempt Christ; but his arts were wasted, he lost the field of battle, and must pay the penalty of defeat. Referring to this, the Lord Jesus said, " I beheld Satan as lightning fall from heaven;" and again, " Now is the prince of of this world cast out;" and again, " The prince of this world is judged."

While, therefore, the opposition which the Christian encounters, the temptations which beset him, the evil against which he must struggle proceed incipiently from the great adversary, it is only the emissaries and agents of the ruler of this world's darkness whom he is called on personally to encounter. As God, in order to save man, must become incarnate in human flesh, so must Satan, in order to tempt, embody himself in some earthly form.

The comforting assurance which Paul administered to the brethren of Corinth was, "There hath no temptation taken you but such as is common [that is, moderated] to man." The work of the Lord Jesus Christ extends some of its blessings to all the race of mankind, to the disobedient as well as to the faithful, and tempers the vicissitudes of our mortal state to our capacity of enduring them. It exempts us, though it did not him, from exposure to Satan's unshackled power. Satan himself is bound and shut up in the pit. God's seal is on him, for he, too, is the property of the divine Being. And he deceives "the nations no more" till the thousand years are fulfilled. Then he is to be "loosed a little season," as we shall see, prior to his overwhelming discomfiture and irretrievable defeat.

2. *Outpouring of the Holy Spirit under the Emblem of Resurrection.*—What has already, in the interpretation of this part of the Apocalypse, been said upon this question will obviate the necessity for any long discussion

of it. Holding the prophecy of Ezekiel in mind, we cannot but conclude that what was meant to be taught by the resurrection of the bones in the valley of vision is likewise indicated by the expression, "They lived and reigned with Christ." "This is the first resurrection." As the resurrection spoken of in Ezekiel was a striking emblem of the power of the Holy Spirit to effect spiritual regeneration, so are the words to be taken here. The usage of describing regeneration by the emblem of a resurrection is so common in the Scriptures that there is no need to adduce illustrations of it. Nor is there any need to dwell upon the analogies between the two or to draw out the important lessons suggested thereby.

One truth, however, is so vital that it must detain us a moment, namely, the absolute necessity for the supernatural agency of the Holy Spirit in the inception of spiritual life. No one who believes in an actual resurrection—that is, in one that is more than figurative and spiritual, in a resurrection which extends to man's complete being, in a resurrection of the body, and not a mere continuance of the life of the soul—conceives that any natural agents in existence, or, at least, within our knowledge, are competent to produce it. The bodies we have here are "terrestrial," brought into and continued in existence by the operation of natural laws. The body of the resurrection, whatever its connection and continuity with the present one, is confessedly "a spiritual body." No forces within the realm of nature are able to create life or to restore it to that which has lost it. The experience and observation of all the centuries fully establish this truth. Whether our present bodies or souls come into existence by traduction or direct creation is another question; but all Christians are agreed that the resurrection of the body must be effected by the direct action of God.

So, likewise, analogy would teach, must it be with regeneration of the soul. That change by which we are raised from the death of sin to the life of God, that transformation by which we cease to be merely citizens of earth and become citizens of heaven, can be effected only by the direct and supernatural agency of the Holy Spirit. No material, earthly, or human forces are sufficiently mighty to bring it to pass. Here God must specifically act—not as in other modes of his work, but by a distinct exercise of power. Nor are we allowed to conceive of entrance into the spiritual kingdom of God as the resultant of any process of evolution or growth; whatever preparation is made for it, the spiritual life of the soul begins in a special operation of the Holy Spirit as specific and distinct as that by which God "breathed into his nostrils the breath of life; and man became a living soul." The closing chapters of the sacred Scriptures are in unison with the opening ones of Genesis, and from the prelude to the final "amen" there is one harmonious melody.

It must be remembered that John was a witness to and a participant in the extraordinary effusion of the Holy Spirit on the day of Pentecost. He speaks, therefore, of that which he knew and testifies to that which he had seen. While the results of the transformation wrought in him are apparent to us, the fact of it was to him a matter of consciousness. It is because he had experienced the power of the Holy Spirit that he declares the necessity for its exercise. And the stress laid upon this regenerating agency of the Spirit in order that we may be made to live and **reign with** Christ is no slight evidence that the man who wrote the Apocalypse and he who recorded the words of Christ, "Except a man be born again, he cannot see the kingdom of God," were one and the same person.

There is no warrant in Scripture for the assumption that the descent of the Holy Ghost upon the band of disciples in Jerusalem was intended to be an anomalous event and incapable of repetition. In the form of manifestation possibly it was, and in the accompanying signs; but not in its spirit and power. Our Lord plainly promised to his disciples the abiding presence of the Comforter to the end of the ages. But that promise was and is conditional. The Holy Ghost was not given until Jesus was glorified, neither can he be now. The recognition and reception of Christ as our only hope and Saviour is the measure according to which the Spirit now imparts his life. Nor can any definition or theory of Christianity be accepted as correct in which the atonement of Christ does not hold the place of central principle. And in proportion as the crucified Christ is believed on and accepted as the only name "given among men, whereby we must be saved," may richer and more abundant outpourings of the Holy Spirit in his offices of regeneration and sanctification be expected.

3. *Union of Christian Believers.*—There is one particular and important item relating to the coming of Messiah's kingdom which is described with greater minuteness and fullness of detail by Ezekiel than by the writer of the Apocalypse. This is the unity of the Church of God—a point upon which the older prophet lays great stress. This unity is set forth both as a direct result of spiritual resurrection and as an essential element of preparation for the final conflict with evil. By symbol and in word he strongly emphasizes the declaration that, as the sticks which he took became one stick in his hand, so should Judah and Ephraim be made one in God's hand. "I will make them one nation. . . . They shall be no more two nations, neither shall they be divided into two kingdoms any more at all." All the wounds of division shall be closed and the scars of schism healed.

It cannot be said that this same truth is so patent in the Revelation, but it is there by justifiable inference. The fact that the saints live and reign with Christ implies that the kingdom is a united one. The union and fellowship of the saints with each other, without division or alienation, is assumed. The obviousness of the truth was sufficient reason for less explicitness of statement. At any rate, if the apostle can be accused of any omission here he made ample amends in the prominence given to the subject in the fourth gospel, in which he records the prayer of our great High Priest, "That they all may be one; as thou, Father, art in me, and I in thee, that they also may be one in us: that the world may believe that thou hast sent me."

The subject which thus opens out to us is one of such absorbing interest as to demand ample consideration. If it be true, as the words of the prophet and, indirectly, of the apostle seem to indicate, that one result of that spiritual quickening by the Holy Spirit called conversion or regeneration is to bring about union between all who call themselves disciples of Christ, then that regeneration cannot be regarded as complete or normal which does not produce fellowship with all other believers; neither can any Church be said to have attained a state in any great degree approaching its ideal which is not in union with the whole Church of Christ. And, in addition, any instrumentalities we may employ in order to bring about the conversion of the world must be ineffectual, or, at least, greatly shorn of their influence, until there exists in the Christian world a unity which finds its example and the source of its power in the divine nature.

Upon this important question there is entire consentience of opinion among the inspired evangelists and apostles of the New Testament. They record their conviction that Caiaphas was speaking as a true prophet of God, however faulty his motives in so doing, when he said that Jesus should die in order to "gather together in one the children of God that were scattered abroad." Appreciating the immense loss of power which had resulted from the schism between Judah and Ephraim, a loss felt even more severely in the moral than in the political world, they strove with all their might to prevent a like division between the Jewish and Gentile converts to Christ. Nor did they cease their efforts, although laying themselves open to the imputation of inconsistency, until finally the matter became one of life or death to Christianity. With a tenacity which appears to us akin to obstinacy, they clung to the hope that the Jewish nation would accept Christ as Messiah and King, that the old Church would, under the transforming power of the Holy Spirit, merge into the new as the dawn melts into the day, and that thus the continuity of history would be preserved.

There can be no question that the rejection of Jesus as Saviour by his own people was a serious disaster. It created a division among those who believed in a living God, a personal Providence, and broke the unity of their testimony in the court of mankind. It sent Christianity out to its work heavily handicapped; and acute opponents, like Celsus and Porphyry, were not slow to avail themselves of the advantage it gave them. Nor has the loss of power therefrom accruing been recovered to this day. The event is sufficient justification for the wise conservatism which marked the actions of the apostles.

As little room can there be now for question that the divided, distracted, segmentary condition of Christendom, with the animosities, envies, sectarianism, undue exaltation of non-essentials, concentration of efforts upon things of minor importance, and cultivation of bigotry caused thereby, operates as a most active factor in shearing the religion of Christ of its legitimate influence. Nor could increase of power within and superiority to the world without be brought about so quickly by any means as by a unity of believers—such unity as the New Testament inculcates. This statement in no degree conflicts with the uniform declaration of the Scriptures that the word of God and the blood of Christ are the two all-important and all-sufficient agencies for the furtherance of the kingdom; it only asserts that the Bible and the cross will not have accomplished their purpose until such unity shall have followed their acceptance.

Paul, the apostle of the Gentiles, no less emphatically affirms with all his authority the necessity of this union. A careful study of his epistles will show that he divides the religious history of the world into three distinct periods—Judaism, Gentilism, and a final period in which these shall be united.

First was Judaism, which began with Abraham, the pioneer and father of such as believe in a living, personal God. It ran its course, fulfilled its mission, and had attained what Paul calls "the fullness of times" when "God sent forth his Son, made of a woman, made under the law, to redeem them that were under the law." The office of Judaism in the rôle of redemption was to bear witness to the supernatural. The Jew believed thoroughly in God as the Creator, the Providence over nature, the Ruler and Judge of mankind; in God as a person distinct from nature and supreme over it. He fully recognized the obligation of the commandment, "The Lord our God is one Lord; and thou shalt love the Lord thy God with all thine heart, and with all thy soul, and with all thy might." But he exalted the supernatural so highly as to put an impassable chasm between God and his creatures. The immanent presence of God in nature was lost sight of in the conception of his transcendency over it. An incarnation of the Deity and, above all, any such contact of God with humanity as to admit of the possibility of his suffering was abhorrent to the mind of the Jew. And so when Christ came to his own as the Word "made flesh" his own received him not.

And, with his foot almost upon the throne of the world, the Jew stumbled and fell.

Following this period, in Paul's conception, was that of Gentilism, which has also its peculiar mission, runs its destined course, and has its times of fullness toward which it tends (Rom. xi, 25). This was also the conception of Christ himself; for he had said, "Jerusalem shall be trodden down of the Gentiles, until the times of the Gentiles be fulfilled" (Luke xxi, 24).

The mission of the heathen Gentilism lay in the sphere of nature and humanity. With all the beauty, grace, order, motion, and life of the world the Gentile was in sympathy. His defect was that he rose no higher. The gods he believed in were simply human and natural forces personified and exalted. His need was to be impressed vividly with the conception of the reality of the supernatural and to recognize the divine Being above and beyond man and the world.

To meet the needs of all classes of humanity God has employed those two great instrumentalities to which reference is so constantly made in the Revelation of St. John—on the one hand, the Bible, the written word, the sword of the Spirit, with its intense realization of the presence and power of God in nature and history; on the other, the cross, the blood of the Lamb, with its rich testimony to the fact that "God so loved the world, that he gave his only begotten Son, that whosoever believeth in him should not perish, but have everlasting life."

It was Paul's confident and inspiring belief that when the fullness of the Gentiles should have come there would be a union of all believers in God; "and so all Israel shall be saved." And this is the truth to which the writer of the Apocalypse bears witness in his vision of the saints who "lived and reigned with Christ" in one united and concordant kingdom.

If, then, the attainment of so desirable and blessed a result as that of the consummation of Christ's kingdom upon earth is contingent upon the unity of believers it surely behooves the disciples of Christ to labor more earnestly than ever before for this unity. The magnitude of the result is worth the sacrifices needed to gain it.

In what this unity shall consist, in what sense believers are to be one, is a question upon which lawful difference of opinion may be allowed, and it is to be settled only by a sympathetic and careful study of the Scriptures. But as to the mode of its attainment and as to what must precede its realization the Bible is sufficiently precise and explict. It will not be secured by a conventional agreement to accept any common and universal symbol, sacrament, or organization; unity means something too vital for that. It will not be founded upon the basis of any past fact, upon any historical creed or institution or order of ministry; unity is something akin to life, and life is progressive, anticipative, not retrospective. The Jewish people were of one common lineage, having the same fathers, the same oracles, the same institutions, but it was by no chain descending from past times that they were held in unity; as soon as the hope of a future Messiah vanished their past associations became a rope of sand.

The Lord Jesus Christ has himself most plainly and authoritatively announced to us the processes by which alone this unity can be attained. In the ever memorable words of his prayer as our great High

Priest he said, "Sanctify them through thy truth: thy word is truth," and then almost immediately added, "That they all may be one." The unity which he anticipated and now desires is one that must be preceded by sanctification. This is fully in accordance with the prophecy of Ezekiel, for the union by which Judah and Ephraim were made one was preceded by the resurrection to life which occurred when the dry and withered bones had been breathed upon by the Spirit. And, in the paragraph of the Apocalypse now under consideration, it was only after the souls of the witnesses and followers of Jesus had been raised by the first resurrection that they lived and reigned with Christ. Nor can any unity be real which is not preceded by a spiritual resurrection from the death of sin into newness of life through the power of the Holy Spirit.

What is here said of unity as applied to the body of believers is equally applicable to each individual. The kingdom of Christ does not reach its designed consummation in the individual until the heart is united to fear the name of the Lord. The exclusion or omission of any part of our composite nature from the sanctifying influences of the Holy Spirit in so far mars the integrity and concord of the kingdom and is below its ideal. Entire sanctification is, as has been said by John Fletcher, a constellation made up by the union of all the graces in a glorious galaxy. And St. Paul teaches us that it is only when we shall "come in the unity of the faith, and of the knowledge of the Son of God," that we shall have attained "unto a perfect man, unto the measure of the stature of the fullness of Christ."

4. *Final Triumph over the Carnal Mind, or Barbarism. Emblem of Gog and Magog.*—With this glorious picture of the outpouring of the Spirit and the complete union of the Church of Christ in his mind, the apostle passes on to the decisive conflict and crowning victory of the kingdom. "When the thousand years are expired," he says, "Satan shall be loosed out of his prison, and shall go out to deceive the nations."

It is worthy of note that the word which is used by St. John for "expired" is the same used in the fourth gospel in several important and significant places, although differently translated. It is found in the prayer of Jesus (John xvii, 23) in connection with the thought of unity, as in the section of the Revelation just considered, and is there rendered "may be made perfect." It is found in the same prayer (John xvii, 4), and is used by our Lord in speaking of his active work upon earth, being there translated "have finished." It is also recorded by St. John as being one of our Lord's exclamations while on the cross (John xix, 30), and is there also rendered "finished."

From these uses of the word the inference is very reasonable that it signifies, not so much the termination of a period of duration, as the completion of a process. The thousand years may be said to have expired, not at the close of any number of years of time, but whenever the ends for which the kingdom of Christ is established are attained. Until those purposes are accomplished the power of Satan is restrained and he is not allowed to exercise the full measure of his strength. He who makes "the wrath of man" to praise him, while "the remainder of wrath" he restrains, guards his Church and his servants as "a garden inclosed."

History and experience furnish many an

example of the providence that shelters and shields the infancy and immaturity of Churches and believers until adult strength has acquired power to resist. The storm that bends the reed will not move the sturdy oak; and one "rooted and grounded in love" can withstand blasts that would be disastrous to the growing and tender shoot. All progress in human laws, in fact, tends to surround the evil-disposed with increasing restraints, in order that the weak and helpless and inexperienced may have an equal chance to develop their individuality.

But at the expiration of this period, we are told, Satan is allowed to go forth to deceive the nations. The writer of the Apocalypse describes the final assault of Satan upon Christ's kingdom under the emblem, so often quoted and so much misunderstood, of Gog and Magog. In so doing he draws again upon Ezekiel; and if we wish to ascertain the meaning of both the apostle and the prophet we must revert to the circumstances under which the prophecy was originally given, and must, in this instance, have recourse to history.

Not long prior to the time of Ezekiel there had occurred a sudden and terrible irruption of barbarians into the civilized parts of the world, which had caused widespread alarm and terror and shaken to its base the fabric of society which had through preceding centuries been laboriously built up. An immense horde of Scythians, in the rudest stage of savagery, without pity or regard for class, sex, age, or condition, with intense contempt for and hatred of those arts of refinement which they were incapable of appreciating, broke loose from their primitive home and, sweeping down through Asia, overwhelming cities and empires, threatened to destroy every vestige of literature, order, and religion and to turn the world back to chaos and anarchy. Happily their onward course was arrested before the injury they caused had become irreparable. From this circumstance the name Gog, which was that of the horde, became the symbol of barbarism, and was used as such both by the prophet of the Old Testament and the apostle of the Revelation.

The truth which is intended to be presented is the possibility of an inroad of that barbarism from which no age is free and from which the most imminent peril to Christianity is to be dreaded. There is in every human being, however civilized, a germ of barbarism, a strain of savagery, which though repressed by education, by culture, or by law, is not destroyed by them, and which under favoring conditions may become the ruling principle of life. In every community of men there will be found some who represent the highest stage which the community has reached; but there will be found some who remain in the most rudimentary condition of barbarism. It is the struggle between these opposing elements which makes the life of the community.

Gog and Magog do not represent heathenism, which is simply a lower form of religion capable of being improved by the increased light of the Gospel. They represent the spirit of barbarism, which opposes itself to every form of religion, lurking as the dark shadow which waits upon all civilization, ready to manifest itself whenever the power which hinders its manifestation relaxes its vigilance. And unhappily there are, even in civilized and Christian countries, institutions allowed to remain whose only result is to foster the tendency toward barbarism, whose purpose is to feed the lower sensual appetites and passions that are at war alike with law, education, culture, and religion, and between which and the kingdom of Christ must be perpetual antagonism until one or the other shall be exterminated. The study of history will reveal the fact that times occur in the life of nations when the tendency to revert to barbarism asserts itself in unusual strength, when the normal movement upward and onward is arrested, and the forces which drag men downward predominate temporarily.

It is such times and conditions of which Satan avails himself to show his most malignant power. With all such tendencies he is in closest alliance, and in the effort to intensify them finds his most congenial employment. It is a mournful fact that the impulse toward the higher and better is not the only one to be found in man or in any creature; we must take into the account the opposite fact of the tendency to revert to lower and baser levels. Indeed, it is not uncommon to notice that an unusual movement in one direction seems to originate an almost equal one in the opposite. Nor can there be any guarantee that the higher and purer faculties shall assert their legitimate sway except in the promised guidance and help of God. In individual experience, even after long and faithful service and growth, there will come at times sudden suggestions and temptations which reveal the existence of desires and passions we had supposed extinct, but which have been kept down only by God's grace and our unceasing watchfulness; such also is the case with the larger aggregations of men into communities and societies. And the price we must pay for liberty is eternal vigilance.

The barbarian is, indeed, a man; the essential elements of humanity lie in him as in all men. But there are properties which belong to the lowest states of society which constitute a differential characteristic and which disappear or, at least, become dormant when growth and culture take place.

The barbarian is an intense realist. He dwells in the region of facts—such facts as are discoverable by his physical nature only. Of sentiment, of ideals, he knows nothing and cares less. Such things as these are spiritually discerned, and he is a natural man only. Of that unseen ether which lies around the bare and bald facts of life, connecting them with the divine and

Progressive Steps

eternal source of things, of those loftier visions of the true, the beautiful, the good which fill the mind of the cultured with intensest delight, he has no conception. His delights and employments are sensual and low, and the end of all of his energies is to gratify them. Arcadian simplicity fades away with increased geographical and ethnological knowledge.

The only forces which the barbarian appreciates, therefore, are the mechanical and physical. With him might is right. Of the power of spiritual forces he has the most inadequate notions until he finds how weak his cunning and artifice are in the presence of civilization. Of that sacrifice and renunciation of self for the sake of love of which the cross of Christ is the summit and crowning example and in which is the demonstration of the power and wisdom of God he is incapable of appreciation until the Holy Spirit breaks the chain with which Satan has bound him; and then he ceases to be a barbarian. Clovis spake the real feeling of the savage, even when baptized, in exclaiming, "Had I been there with my Franks they should not have nailed Jesus to the cross."

By profession the barbarian is a soldier. He knows somewhat of the power of weapons of war and but little else. The mechanical and industrial pursuits by which society is bound together are objects of scorn to him. He has profound contempt for labor as beneath his pride. The aristocracy he admires is built on idleness and bloodshed, not on toil or skill or honest work.

Barbarians divide themselves on national lines alone. The broad humanity which overlaps territorial boundaries, or a patriotism which can embrace all mankind and recognize a universal brotherhood, the barbarian is not able to comprehend, or else he despises the notion as silly and puerile. He has no consideration of any ties save those of kinship, if, indeed, fully of these. All within this limit may not be friends; but certainly all without are enemies, for whose welfare he need have no regard and whose rights he does not recognize.

And because of these things the stage of barbarism is politically that of socialism, of that form of it in which the individual has no value or right of independent thought or action, except as the clan or tribe or community may confer them. The discernment of the real worth of man is the gift of the religion of Jesus. In its teaching that the blood of Christ has been shed for the redemption of all mankind, that the manifestation of the Spirit has been given to everyone, and that, therefore, it is not allowed to call any man common or unclean, it has laid the only solid foundation upon which true liberty, independence, self-respect, and the highest enjoyments of life can be based.

How rife this spirit of barbarism is, even in societies and States called civilized and Christian, a moderate degree of observation will prove. It is to be understood, of course, that to say a tendency exists in mankind to revert to barbarism is far from saying that such a tendency is likely to predominate. In pointing out the dangers which beset civilization the Bible does by no means countenance despondency or encourage doubt as to the future of history. It indicates perils for the purpose of inciting us to the use of the means which it suggests for avoiding them. The spirit of the Bible is one of most cheerful hope as to the outcome of the conflict between good and evil; and nowhere is the tone of assurance stronger than in the Revelation.

But we shall be very unwise if we shall neglect to guard against those symptoms of danger which are manifesting themselves. The persistent attempts to reduce literature and poetry and art to a barbaric realism, dragging into light lusts and passions which modesty, culture, and religion hide from view; the disposition, which seems to increase, to make the boundaries of States and empires coincide with kinship of race, and thus to limit men's interests and aspirations to their own nationalities; the multiplication of armies and the conversion of kingdoms into camps, in which every citizen must be a soldier; the fearful increase of destructive dynamitism and anarchy; the employment of the most advanced science and education in the invention and improvement of machines of war; the growth of that form of socialism which denies all individualism of property, family, and labor—these are indications of that proneness to barbarism from which mankind is not yet free, and from which it will not be free until the world comes into the enjoyment of the liberty of Christ.

Progressive Steps

The keen eye of the apostle discerned, even in the apparently secure age in which he lived, the signs of coming perils and dangers; and against these, men and Churches of all ages have had to struggle. The battle of Christ with Magog is part of that conflict with the carnal man that rages in the heart of every Christian, as well as in the world at large. Happily, however, we know from the pen of inspiration the full measure of danger to be apprehended, and may rest in the assurance that Satan has no other appliances of mischief in reserve when these are exhausted.

It will be noted that the apostle says, in describing the assault of Gog and Magog upon the kingdom of Christ, "They went up on the breadth of the earth, and compassed the camp of the saints about, and the beloved city." A distinction is made between the "city," which symbolizes the Church, and the circumjacent "camp," which is interposed as a bulwark between it and the enemy, and which may be regarded as representing law, education, government, and other conservative forces of the world. There lies in this a thought characteristic of the profound mind of the beloved apostle. In a sense most true and deep, Christians are "the salt of the earth." The interests of humanity are bound up with the welfare of the kingdom. In fighting the battles of God the Church is guarding the welfare of mankind. The bark of Christianity carries man and all his fortunes. Barbarism is the common enemy of government and of religion, and in striving to injure one strikes at the other. Gog and Magog are antagonistic to the "city" and the encircling "camp" alike. In resisting the emissaries and allies of Satan Christianity is struggling for the benefit of civilization and safeguarding all earthly good, even as its Master died not for his own nation only, but for all men dispersed over the globe. For its own sake, if not out of regard for religion, society should jealously prohibit any infringement of divine law. "Happy is that people, whose God is the Lord."

On the other hand, it is a matter of profoundest importance to the cause of religion that it shall maintain the order and prosperity of the community. No Christian can be indifferent to the welfare of the State in which he lives. As he dares not allow himself in his own personal experience to watch without concern any indications of the growth of the carnal mind, neither can he be listless or apathetic when opinions destructive to society are spreading abroad. The attacks upon governments are but the prelude to assaults upon religion. Again and again has "the earth helped the woman," and resistance to lawlessness and anarchy been preservative of the existence of the Church. However far any established government may fall below the ideal, it is yet better than none. "The powers that be are ordained of God," although Nero may wield the scepter. Forms of government are subject to change and may be altered in order to conform to higher ideals; but the existence of government itself is essential to the fulfillment of the purposes of God.

But, however formidable the assault, the apostle does not allow any fears of defeat to eclipse his hope for the future. Victory, however long deferred, is sure to come at last to the Christian and to the Church. "Be of good cheer," the Lord said; "I have overcome the world." The weapons he has put into our hands are amply sufficient for our needs, nor are any agencies necessary beyond those with which he has supplied us.

"Fire came down from God out of heaven, and devoured them." The "fire" here is undoubtedly the fire of the Holy Ghost, the baptism from above of which John the Baptist spake when he said, "He [the Christ] shall baptize you with the Holy Ghost and with fire." There came, it may be, to the apostle, when he wrote these words, memories of an incident of his life (Luke ix, 51–56). In his anger at the inhospitable Samaritans, with a spirit of vindictiveness at the insult to his Master, he had said, "Lord, wilt thou that we command fire to come down from heaven, and consume them, even as Elias did?" How quickly followed the sharp rebuke of the Lord Jesus, "Ye know not what manner of spirit ye are of." The weapons Christ uses are not carnal, but spiritual. The fire which is to devour Gog and Magog is the Holy Spirit who descended upon the Church at Pentecost. The destruction which awaits them is that of their sins and animosity, not of their persons. The Spirit of truth when he comes reproves the world "of judgment, because the prince of this world is judged."

And both the struggle and the victory are for each individual believer, as well as for the Church at large. "We know that whosoever is born of God sinneth not; but he that is begotten of God keepeth himself, and that wicked one toucheth him not." "Ye are of God, little children, and have overcome them: because greater is he that is in you, than he that is in the world."

Thus the consummation to which the apostolic seer looked forward is reached at last. The Lamb into whose hands the dominion of all things was committed has prevailed. He has "put down all rule and all authority and power." "He [that is, God] hath put all things under his feet." Principalities and powers are "subject unto him." He who was lifted up upon the cross is now on the "great white throne." The Father, he himself had said, gave him "authority to execute judgment also, because he is the Son of man." The time of the fulfillment of this promise has come. Death, "the last enemy," is destroyed. The gates of Hades have no longer power to resist the forces of the kingdom of Christ.

Nothing that is hostile to him can look upon his face. Daniel's prophecy has been brought to pass. "The iron, the clay, the brass, the silver, and the gold" are "broken to pieces together," and become "like the chaff of the summer threshing floors;" and the wind has "carried them away," that no place is "found for them." The kingdom which the God of heaven has set up has consumed all other kingdoms and stands for ever (Dan. ii, 35, 44; vii, 13, 14).

But there is one thought developed in the closing paragraph of chapter xx which deserves a moment's consideration. It is that in the relation which men and things sustain to the Lord Jesus Christ lies the true test of character and the standard of future, as well as present judgment. "Set for the fall and rising again of many in Israel," through him "the thoughts of many hearts" are revealed (Luke ii, 34, 35). He is, as has been aptly said, the touchstone of human hearts. And it will be by the "inasmuch as ye did" or "did it not" unto him that the final sentence on men will be determined.

This truth is set forth in the expression, "the book of life." "Whosoever was not found written in the book of life was cast into the lake of fire." In the prophecy of Daniel, to which there is evidently reference in this paragraph, mention is made of "books" that "were opened." The writer of the Apocalypse also alludes to the "books" that "were opened." But he adds to this that "another book was opened, which is the book of life;" and in chapter xxi, 27, he calls it "the Lamb's book of life." It is apparent that this additional standard of judgment belongs to the New Testament dispensation and is something having relation to the specific work of the Lord Jesus Christ. Paul has this in mind in saying (1 Cor. xvi, 22), "If any man love not the Lord Jesus Christ, let him be Anathema Maran-atha." The Saviour had given a foreshadowing of the same truth in telling his disciples, "Whosoever therefore shall confess me before men, him will I confess also before my Father which is in heaven." We hear an echo of this in the epistle to Sardis (Rev. iii, 5): "He that overcometh, the same shall be clothed in white raiment; and I will not blot out his name out of the book of life, but I will confess his name before my Father, and before his angels." The same truth is indicated by John in his first epistle (1 John v, 12): "He that hath the Son hath life; and he that hath not the Son of God hath not life."

The character of men is not to be estimated solely by their actions, and to make destiny depend upon them would hardly be just. Every act, whether of word or deed, has its own standard of judgment. That which determines its quality as good or bad is its fitness or unfitness to its designed end; in this consists its conformity with its ideal. A moral agent has, however, another standard of judgment. Goodness or badness in his case is determined by the conformity of his motives, purposes, and intentions with his ideal, which is the fulfillment of the will of his Creator. Not only what he does, but why he does it, enters into the estimate of his moral character. A perfect man would be one in whom faith in the Son of God and experimental knowledge of him are in unison, one whose conduct springs out of a living faith, and in whom a correct faith is translated into actual and complete righteousness of conduct.

It is a fact that upon the fundamental principles of ethics the great religions of the earth do not differ so much from each other as presumption leads us to anticipate. This agreement of the moral codes occasions surprise and even perplexity upon the first appreciation of the fact. But the explanation is simple and easy. These codes are largely the result of observation upon the established and permanent laws of the universe, deductions from facts with which testimony, reason, and consciousness make men acquainted. The data being the same, the conclusions reached are closely similar.

It is the motive power which they bring to bear upon men in order to induce them to actual realization of and conformity to their moral convictions that determines the superiority or inferiority of religions. That which constitutes the distinguishing characteristic of Christianity and gives it its immense preëminence over all other forms of religious belief is that it reveals to us the cross of Christ as the greatest motive power that can operate in human nature. To depreciate or ignore the atonement is to leave out the differentiating element of the religion of Jesus. "He that believeth on the Son hath everlasting life: and he that believeth not the Son shall not see life · but the wrath of God abideth on him"

(John iii, 36). "We must all be made manifest before the judgment seat of Christ; that each one may receive the things done in the body" (2 Cor. v, 10, Revised Version). Wherever, indeed, the full revelation of the Lord Jesus Christ has not been given to men they are to be judged by "the law written in their hearts, their conscience also bearing witness" (Rom. ii, 15). But where the revelation has been made it is in likeness to him that the test of character lies. And for the final determination of destiny there must be, not only the books of words and deeds, but also the "Lamb's book of life."

PART VII

The Ideal of the Kingdom

PART VII
The Ideal of the Kingdom

By these long steps has the holy apostle brought us, through this wonderful record of perils, conflicts, defeats, victories, judgments, and blessings, to the conclusion toward which he has from the commencement been tending; and in the two chapters which close the book he depicts the ideal and perfect kingdom of Christ as it appeared in his conception of it. As Ezekiel in his lonely captivity by the Chebar was comforted with anticipations of a new Canaan and a new temple, wherein Israel, purified by its sufferings and cleansed from idolatry, should enjoy renewed and uninterrupted communion with Jehovah, so was the exiled apostle of Patmos gladdened with a prophetic foresight of new heavens and a new earth in which righteousness shall dwell, not as a wayfarer or one that tarrieth for a night, but as a permanent and eternal inhabitant. For the instruction of all the generations to follow John presents his inspired conception of what the kingdom of Christ in its purest and final form is, whether it be conceived as existing in the heart of an individual believer, or as synonymous with the Church, the body of believers.

We are certainly not compelled, and it may seriously be questioned whether we are allowed, to interpret the concluding chapters of the Apocalypse as a vision of the future heaven which awaits the just, of the glorified and celestial state of believers who have passed through the trials of earth and have entered into their final reward. The probabilities are very strong that it is rather the vision of a redeemed and purified earth, the victory which shall result here from the complete ascendancy of Christ, which is presented to our faith and hope. This interpretation of the vision would give consistency and unity to the book. It would account for the discrimination which is certainly made between the "city" and the nations which "walk in the light thereof," and also for the statement that the leaves of the tree of life are "for the healing of the nations;" and it is confirmed by the fact that in his first epistle, which was probably written subsequently to the Apocalypse, John declared that it had not been revealed

The Ideal of the Kingdom

or made manifest to him at that time what we shall be when Christ shall be manifested to us in his heavenly glory (1 John iii, 2)— a statement hardly to be reconciled with truth if the vision of the Apocalypse is to be taken as a revelation of the heavenly state.

The careful student will not fail to observe that upon all questions relating to the life beyond the grave the Bible preserves a marked reticence; nor is there any more impressive evidence of its divinity than this. To gratify a curiosity which might easily become morbid is no part of its object and might defeat its more practical purpose. While, therefore, it shows us the rent veil and opens the curtain sufficiently to reveal to us a world lying beyond, it does not allow us to penetrate further or uncover to us the mysteries hidden therein. It is enough for us to know that a way leads from the holy place to the holy of holies, and that Christ is that way, the life of the world beyond as he is of this, and the truth and reality of both alike. It is not certain that a revelation to us of the glories of the celestial state would realize to us the satisfaction we anticipated. Even were a revelation made to us in terms which we were able to grasp and comprehend, that which would be blissful to our glorified and transformed faculties might not seem so to our earthly ones, and the revelation might become rather a stumbling-block than a stimulus. We know that the prophecies concerning the Messiah in the Old Testament were not only obscure, but even seemed to involve contradictions, which, however, his advent in the flesh explained and reconciled. This may be the case also in regard to the future state of the blessed. And God is no less merciful, doubtless, in what he withholds than in what he imparts.

It is the ideal kingdom of Christ here in its perfect and completed form, and not the glorified realm above, which John so exquisitely describes. The imagery he uses to adumbrate it may be glowing, but it is not beyond what may be gathered, though in less poetic dress, from other parts of the Scriptures. Even should it be conceded that the picture is simply an ideal one, a dream of beauty not meant to be realized, in fact, something the attainment of which lies beyond the possibilities of this mortal life, still the presentation to us of the per-

The Ideal of the Kingdom

fect state can not be without its uses of help and comfort.

But it was not the cast of John's mind to be pleased with imagined fancies. It has been well said (in *Guesses at Truth*) that "in character, in affection, the ideal is the only real." It is not without reason that John has so elaborately described the agencies with which Christ has so amply endowed his Church and his disciples, and which are sufficient, if rightly used, to reduce to actual experience all that is portrayed as ideal.

In one of those graphic sketches which connect the Apocalypse so closely with the gospels John convinces us that it is fact, and not fancy, which has been engaging his pen. At the beginning of his ministry upon earth Christ, we are told, was taken to "an exceeding high mountain," whence "all the kingdoms of the world, and the glory of them," were shown him; and Satan said to him, "All these things will I give thee, if thou wilt fall down and worship me." From this temptation the Master recoiled with indignant rebuke. Instead thereof, he chose deliberately the path of suffering and privation, the path that led to the garden and the cross, to Gethsemane and Calvary. With full appreciation of all it involved, he took the cup put into his hands by the Father. In the closing scenes of the Apocalypse the battle is supposed to have been fought, the conflict has ceased, and now John himself stands, as Christ had stood, upon "a great and high mountain;" and, behold, there was shown him "that great city, the holy Jerusalem, descending out of heaven from God." The cross has conquered, and the kingdoms of the earth have become the possession of our Lord and of his Christ. And he who himself overcame the world has given assurance to all his followers, however humble, that they, too, may be victors.

Theories of the Church and kingdom of Christ, definitions of their nature and mission, abound. Many have taken on them to specify the notes or characteristic marks by which the true Church may be identified. It cannot, therefore, fail of interest or profit to learn what the holy St. John, the inspired apostle who leaned on the bosom of Jesus, has to say of the tests by which we may try the spirits to see whether they are of God. Under the veil of figure and metaphor, we have the profound and

The Ideal of the Kingdom

long-studied conviction of one who was competent to decide, and to whom the wisest of mankind may look up with reverence for instruction. Nor need anyone have difficulty in determining for himself whether the kingdom of Christ finds its realization in his own soul, or long hesitate in identifying the true Church of Christ, which is simply the kingdom of Christ ruling in society.

1. *The Distinctive Features of the Kingdom.*—The first mark of the kingdom upon which John lays stress is that it is supernatural in its origin. The holy city that he saw descended "out of heaven from God." It came "down from God out of heaven, prepared as a bride adorned for her husband." It is not the resultant of any process of development or growth from a prior state. Whatever preparation may precede and make ready a basis for its reception, the kingdom itself is inaugurated by the direct and personal agency of the Holy Spirit. Whatever instrumentalities the Holy Ghost may use as his media, his is the undivided quickening power. In this declaration the writer of the Apocalypse and the author of the fourth gospel are in agreement. It is

he who records the words of the Lord Jesus, "Except a man be born of water and of the Spirit, he cannot enter into the kingdom of God" (John iii, 5).

Another feature of this kingdom is that its mission lies specifically in the realm of divine things. It has "the glory of God." The name of the city is, "The Lord is there" (Ezek. xlviii, 35). Its God is its glory. It is God's witness in nature and to men of a power above and beyond nature and man. There are natural means and agencies endowed by the Creator to carry forward earthly work; but he has planted the kingdom in the midst of mankind, and its one great business is to testify of him. For the doing of this work the Church is accountable. In whatever other tasks the Church may engage or whatever methods it may employ in fulfilling its mission, its one supreme office and distinct characteristic is to bear witness to a divine presence and a divine power in the world. "In his temple doth everyone speak of his glory." All art, ritual, discipline, philanthropy, and economies that do not directly lead to God, and have not for their purpose to emphasize the need, the presence, and the inward experience of the supernatural, are aside from the purpose of the kingdom and below its ideal.

A third mark of the kingdom is that it has to do primarily with the religious faculties. As the distinction between nature and the supernatural is permanent and ineffaceable, so the Church and the world can never be made to coincide, however widely the Church may be extended or however thoroughly the world may be permeated by the spirit of the Church. "The nations of them which are saved shall walk in the light" of the new Jerusalem, "the kings of the earth do bring their glory and honor into it;" but the distinction between it and them exists and abides. It will be as true in the last days as when our Lord first spoke the words, "My kingdom is not of this world." However omnipotent and omnipresent God may be in nature and the universe, he can never be made identical with them; and, however thoroughly they may be penetrated by his Spirit and come to perfect accord with him, they can never be so lifted up as to rival or supersede his supremacy. And, although common life and work may be sanctified by being done in the spirit of Christ, and religious life may flow out from the central source through all the ordinary and natural channels of our being, the religious and the secular can never be made one. "Out of Zion shall go forth the law, and the word of the Lord from Jerusalem;" but the discharge of earthly duties and the reformation of earthly conditions can never exhaust the obligations of man. There will still remain those relations to the supernatural of whose existence and sovereignty it is the preëminent mission of the Church to testify. The kingdom of God is "righteousness, and peace, and joy in the Holy Ghost."

2. *The Central Principle of the Kingdom.*—The central figure in this kingdom is Christ crucified. It is the Lamb around whom all the imagery of the apostle's description gathers. The light—luminary, rather—of the kingdom was "like unto a stone most precious, even like a jasper stone, clear as crystal." That this refers to Christ seems probable from Rev. iv, 3, where it is said that he that sat upon the throne "was to look upon like a jasper and a sardine stone," and is further confirmed by Rev. xxi, 23, where the Lamb is said to

The Ideal of the Kingdom

be "the light" of the city. Moreover, it is said, "The first foundation was jasper," which is but confirmatory of what Peter had said in the presence of John to the "rulers, and elders, and scribes: " "This is the stone which was set at nought of you builders, which is become the head of the corner. Neither is there salvation in any other." (Acts iv, 11, 12.)

Still further, "The building of the wall of it was of jasper." Christ crucified is the defense and the bulwark of the kingdom. The atonement of Christ is the most powerful argument the Church can use and constitutes its strongest claim upon the reason and heart of men. It is "the power of God, and the wisdom of God." It is Christ crucified that makes the separation between the kingdom and the circumjacent world. It is not in its ethics that the distinguishing peculiarity of Christianity lies, but in the preaching of the cross. In the opinion of John any other definition of Christianity throws down Christianity's only wall of safety and separation.

Yet there is no exclusiveness about the kingdom. The city has three gates on each of its four sides, facing the four quarters of the globe, that all men may find ready access. "Every several gate is of one pearl"—that pearl of great price which Christ said a man should be willing to sell all that he has to buy, becoming eternally rich by the exchange.

Nor is there any narrowness. Its length and breadth and height exceed even those large measurements which Ezekiel thought to be ample enough for the ideal temple he saw. "Whatsoever things are true, whatsoever things are honest, whatsoever things are just, whatsoever things are pure, whatsoever things are lovely, whatsoever things are of good report; if there be any virtue, and if there be any praise"—all these things belong legitimately to the kingdom. The kings of the earth may "bring their glory and honor into it;" only that which "defileth" or "worketh abomination" or "maketh a lie" is excluded. When once a man in the center of his being is rightly adjusted to the Lamb of God, the center of all being, he may unfold all his powers and give exercise to every faculty of his renewed nature safely, wisely, completely, without fear of infringement upon any other being or of going astray from his Creator.

The Ideal of the Kingdom

3. *Negative Characteristics.*—Not less remarkable is the negative side of the kingdom, the absence from it of many things with which we are familiar. When an ideal has been attained much that was necessary in the process of attainment falls away as obsolete; the scaffolding which is used in the erection of a building is removed when the building is completed.

There is a noticeable avoidance in the closing chapters of the Apocalypse of any reference to the sacraments, to ritual, or to such like means of grace. John saw "no temple therein; for the Lord God Almighty and the Lamb are the temple of it." "When that which is perfect is come, then that which is in part shall be done away." When the consummation of the kingdom has been reached the relation of the soul to its Creator shall not be through intermediate agencies, but direct and intuitive.

There is no mention made of any special priestly class, for the promise shall have its complete fulfillment to all, "Ye are a chosen generation, a royal priesthood;" and all life shall be a priestly work and service.

Nor is there any allusion to the prophetic

office as a separate function. "They need no candle, neither light of the sun; for the Lord God giveth them light." "The anointing which ye have received of him abideth in you, and ye need not that any man teach you" (1 John ii, 27). The prediction of Jeremiah (Jer. xxxi, 34) has reached its time of fulfillment: "They shall teach no more every man his neighbor, and every man his brother, saying, Know the Lord: for they shall all know me, from the least of them unto the greatest of them, saith the Lord.'

Yet upon this point, more almost than upon any other, it is of the utmost importance that we shall "distinguish the times." We must not assume, because these aids and appliances are not needful in the perfected state of the kingdom, that they are not essential in the formative period, and thus, at great risk and with imminent peril, neglect or depreciate those means of grace which the Creator has deemed necessary for our present condition.

4. *The Fruits and Results of the Kingdom.* —They in whom the kingdom rules shall have access to the tree of life, that heavenly wisdom of which Solomon says, "She is a

The Ideal of the Kingdom

tree of life to them that lay hold upon her: and happy is everyone that retaineth her" (Prov. iii, 18). "This is life eternal," One greater than Solomon says, "that they might know thee the only true God, and Jesus Christ, whom thou hast sent" (John xvii, 3). Their lives shall abound in fruitfulness. Their ministry shall be, like the Lord's, "for the healing of the nations," a remedy for all the spiritual and earthly maladies of mankind.

The curse of sin shall be destroyed, "and there shall be no more curse." "Christ hath redeemed us from the curse of the law, being made a curse for us" (Gal. iii, 13). "The blood of Jesus Christ his Son cleanseth us from all sin" (1 John i, 7). And walking "in the light, as he is in the light," and being "pure in heart," his followers shall "see God." "They shall see his face; and his name shall be in their foreheads."

Thus with this sublime vision closes this marvelous book. There is no truth revealed elsewhere in the sacred Scriptures that may not be found in its pages. So complete is it, indeed, that "if any man shall add unto these things, God shall add unto him the plagues that are written in this book." Nor is there any truth revealed in this book which may not be found elsewhere in the Scriptures, so perfectly does it harmonize with all divinely inspired truth. Therefore, "if any man shall take away from the words of the book of this prophecy, God shall take away his part out of the book of life, and out of the holy city, and from the things which are written in this book."

The Apocalypse of St. John fitly closes the sacred canon; for, drawing so much, as it does, from all the rest of God's wonderful book, it holds the truths derived therefrom in a coherent union never to be dissolved or broken.

Index

Albigenses, 137.
Apocalypse. See Revelation.
Apostolic and present age, resemblance between, 198.
Asceticism and worldliness contrasted, 148-150.
Asceticism, prevalence and danger of, 138, 139.
Atonement, all-sufficiency of, 164, 165.
Babylon, destruction of, 199.
    relation of Church and State in, 179-181.
Balaam, 147, 148.
Barbarism, characteristics of, 244-247.
    possibility of reversion to, 74, 75, 243.
Beast, scarlet colored, 186-188.
Bible, reticence of, 263.
Christ crucified, the central figure of Revelation, 270, 171.
Christian liberty, 272.
Christianity, antithesis between true and false, 184, 185.
Church and State, interdependence of, 110, 249, 250.
Church, conquering weapons of the, 110, 155, 202.
    the ideal, 266, *ff*.
    notes of the true, 266, *ff*.
    separable from world, 269, 270.
    supernatural origin of the, 267.
    a witness to God, 268.
Church unity, 228, *ff*.
    an apostolic hope, 230, 231.
    how attained, 236, 237.
    importance of, 232.
Daniel, prophecy of four beasts in, 115.
David, duration of dynasty of, 209.

Index

Dragon, the; divine protection from, 108.
   hostility of, to the church, 107.
Dry bones. *See* Ezekiel, vision of dry bones.
Emblem, of seal, 39–41.
   of trumpet, 56, 57.
Epistles to seven churches of Asia, their lesson to us, 34.
Euphrates, reference to, in sixth trumpet, 72, 73.
Ezekiel, prophecy of, 163, 164, 205, *ff.*
   vision of dry bones, 207, 208.
False prophet, marks of, 133.
False prophetism, second wild beast a symbol of, 126.
Fifth trumpet. *See* Trumpet fifth.
First trumpet. *See* Trumpet first.
Forty-two, symbolism of, 19.
Fourth trumpet. See Trumpet fourth.
Gentilism, mission of, 234.
Gnosticism perilous to Christianity, 136.
God, knowledge of; how obtained, 59–61.
Gog and Magog, 209, 240–243, 252, 253.
Harvest scene, meaning of, 157–159.
Holy Spirit, his work preceded by that of Christ, 141, 142.
Individuality an outgrowth of Christianity, 134, 135.
Inspiration and human genius, 84.
Interpretation, principles of, 10.
   reference to Old Testament necessary in, 13–16.
   structure of book a guide to, 11–13.
Jewish ritual a key to emblems and symbols, 16.
Joel, prophecy of, 155–157.
Judaism, its office in the plan of redemption, 233.
Knowledge of God through his works and word, 59–61.
Lamb's book of life, 254, *ff.*
Lukewarmness, evils of, 69, 70.
Man and the earth, close connection between, 63, 64.
Manichæism, 137.
Mediatorial sovereignty, 45, 46, 214.
Michael the archangel, 109.
Millennium, 211, 212, 217, 218.

Index

Mohammedanism illustrative of fifth trumpet, 70, 71.
Nicolaitanes, 136.
Nineveh, special characteristics of, 178, 179.
Numbers, importance of, 17.
Old Testament, its relation to the New, 93-95.
    reference to it necessary in interpretation, 13-16.
Palestine, geographical seclusion of, 108, 109.
Paulicianism, 137.
Peculiarities distinguishing the Revelation, 9.
Plagues, the, 170.
Prophetical books, importance of study of, 14.
Purpose of the Revelation, 9.
Resurrection, spiritual, 224, 225.
Revelation, general purpose of the, 9.
    limitations of the, 81, 82.
    theme of the, 23.
    unity of the, 22.
Roman Empire, policy of administration, 117, 118.
Rome, Church of, 192, 193.
Sacraments, absence of allusion to, 273.
Satan, his power restrained, 219.
    loosing of, 238.
Sea, emblem of secular world, 113.
Seal, emblematic meaning of, 39-41.
    loosing of, 44.
Sealed book, meaning of, 41, 42.
Sealed elect, 50-52.
Second trumpet. *See* Trumpet second.
Second wild beast, number of, 142-148.
Seven churches of Asia, spiritual condition of, 30.
Seven seals, opening of, 46.
Seven, symbolism of, 18.
Seventh trumpet. *See* Trumpet seventh.
Simon Magus, 136.
Six, symbolism of, 19.
Sixth trumpet. *See* Trumpet sixth.
Theme of the Revelation, 23.

Index

Third trumpet. *See* Trumpet third.
Three and a half, symbolism of, 19-22.
Tree of life, 274, 275.
True prophet, marks of, 129-131.
Trumpet, emblematic meaning of, 56, 57.
    fifth, explanation of, 67-71.
    first, explanation of, 65.
    fourth, explanation of, 66.
    second, explanation of, 65.
    seventh, explanation of, 97.
    sixth, explanation of, 72-76.
    third, explanation of, 66.
Twelve, symbolism of, 18.
Twelve hundred and sixty, symbolism of, 19, 88, 109.
Two witnesses, interpretation of, 79.
Tyre, deleterious influence upon religion, 182, 183.
    emblem of commerce, 181, 182, 195, 196.
Unity of the church. *See* Church unity.
Vials, vision of, 169.
Victory, anticipation of, 150.
Vintage scene, meaning of, 159-165.
Witnesses, the two ; fulfilled in Law and Prophets, 87-92.
Woes, the three, 76.
World empires, 189.
    recurrence of, impossible, 191.
World religions, agreement of moral codes, 256, 257.
Worldliness and asceticism contrasted, 148-150.
Worldliness, blasphemy of, 123, 124.
    definition of, 120.
    first wild beast, a symbol of, 112.
    recuperative power of, 122.

www.ingramcontent.com/pod-product-compliance
Lightning Source LLC
Chambersburg PA
CBHW031928230426
43672CB00010B/1856